The
POTTY MOUTH
at the
TABLE

The
POTTY MOUTH
at the
TABLE

LAURIE NOTARO

G

GALLERY BOOKS

New York   London   Toronto   Sydney   New Delhi

Gallery Books
A Division of Simon & Schuster, Inc.
1230 Avenue of the Americas
New York, NY 10020

First Gallery Books trade paperback edition April 2013

GALLERY BOOKS and colophon are registered trademarks of Simon & Schuster, Inc.

For information about special discounts for bulk purchases, please contact Simon & Schuster Special Sales at 1-866-506-1949 or business@simonandschuster.com.

The Simon & Schuster Speakers Bureau can bring authors to your live event. For more information or to book an event contact the Simon & Schuster Speakers Bureau at 1-866-248-3049 or visit our website at www.simonspeakers.com.

Designed by Jaime Putorti

Manufactured in the United States of America

10 9 8 7 6 5 4 3 2

Library of Congress Cataloging-in-Publication Data

Notaro, Laurie
   The potty mouth at the table / Laurie Notaro. — First Gallery Books trade paperback edition.
       p. cm.
1. Notaro, Laurie. 2. Etiquette—Humor. 3. Humorists, American—20th century—Biography. 4. American wit and humor. I. Title.
   PS3614.O785Z476 2013
   814'.6—dc23
   [B]   2012039338

ISBN 978-1-4516-5939-9
ISBN 978-1-4516-5941-2 (ebook)

To the bravest of them all,
Kartz Ucci

CONTENTS

CONTENTS

The
POTTY MOUTH
at the
TABLE

ANTIQUES NO SHOW

Turn that off!" I yelled to my husband from my office as soon as I heard the old-timey music broadcast from the television. My husband knew better, and I mumbled that as I heard him scramble for the remote control and then abruptly change the channel.

"I hate them!" I called out for emphasis. "Go to hell, *Antiques Roadshow*! Go to hell!"

My husband then flipped to what sounded like a woman screaming as she was being covered with tarantulas. "Do you prefer this?" he asked, turning up the volume.

"Yes," I replied adamantly. "I don't ever want to hear that stupid-ass flute played in this house again."

"I think it's a clarinet," he corrected me. "It's definitely from the woodwind family."

"I don't care what it is!" I screeched. "I would rather be standing in the hall in my underwear and hear your mom's voice right behind me than hear that song again! Hustlers! Grifters! Swindlers! Mountebanks!"

In the next second, my husband's head popped into the doorway of my office.

"Do you really hate them so much that you went to thesaurus.com to come up with new words to toss out in your *Antiques Roadshow* rages?" he asked candidly.

"What would you call them if they did that to you?" I demanded. "Malefactors!"

"You're pronouncing that wrong," he informed me, then disappeared back into the living room.

"I am archenemies with them!" I shouted after him. "It's part of our nemesis-ial relationship!"

I didn't always hate *Antiques Roadshow.* I used to like it. In fact, when it was announced that the show was coming to Eugene, I could hardly contain my excitement. I had waited for this opportunity for years, *years,* and I felt a little thrill in my chest every single time I thought about it. Because I had something *good.* Really good. So good that I knew: I would get not only on the show with a treasure like this, but on previews as well. So good that it might just make *Antiques*

Roadshow history and end up in a museum with its own security guard.

Yes, it was that good.

Let me first say that I am cheap. It's true. If I can't buy something wholesale or at least at a significant discount, I will track down that deal like it's the last piece of cake at a Weight Watchers meeting. I've spent inordinate amounts of time doing this. My bargain-hunting record? Three years of searching eBay until I got the Marc Jacobs lace-up suede boots for twenty-three percent of what they cost retail. *In my size.* That was until 2009, when my ten-year search for W. S. George antique coffee mugs was completed when I paid twelve dollars for a dozen of new old stock.

In that same lucky antiques store where I found the mugs, I spied a big art nouveau poster propped up in the corner and half-hidden by shadows. It was a beaut. Six feet tall, printed on copper foil, and mounted on a giant sheet of plywood—a poster for *Lorenzaccio,* a play starring Sarah Bernhardt, that was signed "Mucha." Immediately, I hooked both of my chubby arms around it and dragged it to the front counter, knocking over a dress form and nearly shattering a mirror.

The shop owner informed me that Mucha was an important artist, the father of Art Nouveau, and that this poster came from a turn-of-the-century theater in central California that had been torn down half a century ago. The poster, one of several, had hung in the lobby behind glass, according to the person who had kept them in storage until the antiques dealer happened upon this one and brought it to her store.

And now it had my fingerprints all over it, slightly damp ones (there was mayonnaise on my sandwich at lunch). I knew that if I played my cards right, and this poster was original, it could make up for the fact that I had contributed more to my shoe collection than to my 401(k) account, the consequence of hastily scribbled odds of my rate of butter consumption vs. reaching retirement age. And for the record, I paid less for the poster than for my car payment.

I got the poster home and propped it up in my living room, and over the next couple of months, I went to work and did some research, e-mailed numerous galleries and art appraisers for any hints on whom I should contact or talk to next about my Mucha. I explained what I knew about its origins, included photos, and then I waited. And waited. And waited. I'm still waiting. I took that as a sign that something of this caliber was so rare that it automatically threw a shadow of doubt on its own pedigree, and that something like it simply had never been seen before.

Every year or two since I brought the piece home, I did

additional research on my Mucha, e-mailed a new art gallery or poster dealer, but the result was always the same: nothing. I even e-mailed *History Detectives,* one of my favorite shows, which investigates the history and authenticity of certain objects, and to my surprise, a producer called me back. I was elated and couldn't wait for the investigation to begin but was subsequently informed that the research team ran into a dead end. After speaking to the antiques dealer I bought the piece from, they couldn't find any further information about the origins of the piece, either. I was disappointed to hear the news and flopped on the couch to sulk.

"Maybe this is a sign that the poster should remain a mystery," my husband suggested. "Maybe if you did find out anything about it, you could be opening a can of worms. Before you know it, Prague could be on our answering machine claiming that they want their poster back and that the mustardy fingerprints under your mayonnaise ones belonged to the Nazis. Especially if the show assigned you to Elyse Luray; it would be better to get Gwen Wright. She could keep a secret, I think."

"I love Gwen," I interjected with a smile. "But yes, Elyse would be on the phone to Prague in a second."

Don't get me wrong, I never want to benefit from Nazi plunder, but if I didn't know that my poster had been stolen by greedy fascists, then it couldn't be my fault if it was still hanging on my wall, where I got to gaze at it every day and love democracy.

So I let it go. I stopped searching and accepted the poster for what it was: an unknown . . . until years later. I was reading the newspaper one day and saw that *Antiques Roadshow* was coming to my town. Suddenly, I felt a flutter in my chest, almost certain that it was a butter-clogged artery. *And a sign.*

I needed to go, I decided. I had to go. *I was going to go.*

But deciding to go to *Antiques Roadshow* and actually being able to go are two completely different things, like the difference between what's on Mickey Rourke's face and the skin on the rest of humanity. Apparently, many, many people believe they have historical treasures of utmost significance hanging above their plaid La-Z-Boys in their rec rooms or growing rust in their gardens, so many that you don't just "get" tickets to the show.

Instead, you get a lottery number. I was initially fine with that. I mean, really, I don't live in a very big town, so I felt my chances were good to excellent. So I submitted my name and address on the *Antiques Roadshow* website.

Of course I was going to get tickets.

I was going to get tickets.

And when I told my friend Ariane about it, she replied with delight that she had something she'd like to have appraised, too, and that we should make a pact: if I got tickets, I would take her, and if she got tickets, she would take me. We both doubled our chances in a second and I already had the tape measure out to figure how to get the poster in my car.

And then we waited for the date that they would send us our "Congratulations, Laurie, Your Mucha Poster, the Greatest Find in *Antiques Roadshow* History, Is About to Be Authenticated!" e-mail.

And waited. And waited.

"Did you hear anything?" I'd call Ariane and ask.

"No, did you?" she'd reply.

"No," I'd answer sadly.

"We will," she'd assure me.

"Oh, I know," I'd confirm. "We're going."

And just to make sure, I checked every week to see that I had the date right and how much closer we were getting. I couldn't stand it. I thought about buying a new dress to wear, because certainly this would be highlighted not only on the show itself but also in commercials and trailers and most likely on the website, too. I practiced my expression of utter joy and couldn't decide whether I should cry softly or be graciously stunned by the wonderment of it all. Both looks were good, so I decided that I'd go with whatever felt more genuine in the moment.

Oh, I thought, I hope I get a twin! I don't care which one. They're both equally creepy. Even though they look the same, I have a feeling they each might elicit a different prepared reaction from me.

I looked at the Mucha, knowing that soon it was going to be legitimized, verified, respected for what it was. It was essential that its pedigree was finally recognized, especially after escaping the wrecking ball and being kept in storage for half a century.

The day that the ticket winners were notified, I woke up early and checked my e-mail.

Nothing.

I went to the *Antiques Roadshow* website and put in my confirmation number. The screen came up blank. I had not been chosen.

I texted Ariane as soon as I saw the sun crest over my neighbor's roof.

Laurie Notaro 7:46 a.m.

I didn't get tickets. :(Did you? Did you e-mail me? I'll check again. Nope. Nothing? What about you? No. Still nothing!

Laurie Notaro 7:48 a.m.

Hello? Hello? I thought you got up at 7. Check your e-mail! Anxious! Like a little hard to breathe.

Laurie Notaro 7:51 a.m.

What time do you get up? Don't you have to be at work? Is your connection down? Because I know you are good with paying bills. Ha-ha! Seriously, I'm getting dizzy.

Laurie Notaro 7:55 a.m.

Wake up! Please! THIS IS AN EMERGENCY!

Laurie Notaro 7:59 a.m.

If you take someone else, I will need my shoes back. I know I said my feet are too wide for them, but I am sure I can get them to fit with a layer of baby oil. We had a deal.

Laurie Notaro 8:21 a.m.

Fine. Leave them on my porch.

And then, like magic, I got an e-mail from *Antiques Roadshow*. My eyes got watery. My heart fluttered as if I had eaten a cookie too fast. Oh, thank God, I sighed. They made a mistake. Thank God. I knew I couldn't get those shoes on unless I had a saw.

I clicked on the e-mail quickly, sitting up in my chair in front of the computer, and as the e-mail loaded, my eyes darted over the message and I bit my lip.

Deeeeep breath.

"What's on?" the e-mail asked me.

"Us??" I hoped in a tiny voice. "Us! Us! Us!"

"Biloxi, Hr 1—TONIGHT at 8/7C PM," the e-mail continued. "In Biloxi, Mark L. Walberg and appraiser David Rago check out the wild pottery of George Ohr. . . ."

It was a newsletter. *Antiques Roadshow,* those scoundrels, those filthy, terrible knaves, had sent me a newsletter on the day they had decided to deny me tickets.

It was savage.

I didn't hear from Ariane until later that night, after I had calmed down and drank some wine; she had left her phone at home and called right after she saw that I was stalking her, and by now she probably thought I was standing outside her bedroom window with my iPhone in hand, waiting for her to hand over some strappy wedges.

"I have bad news. I checked my number, too," she said sadly. "I didn't get tickets, either. And, um, I'm wearing the shoes, so . . . ?"

"It's all right," I slurred, trying to be a good sport through my increasing drunkenness. "I'd really have to sever half of my toes to get those things buckled. I'm bummed about the tickets, but at least we tried. I still can't believe we didn't get them. I wonder how many tickets those *Antiques Roadshow* varlets gave out?"

"Well, I have more bad news," Ariane added. "We didn't

get tickets, but my neighbor, who didn't even know about *Antiques Roadshow* coming here until I told her, got tickets, and has no idea what to bring, except a carved frog she got in Mexico."

"Ohmygodihateeugene," I said in one syllable. "Would she—"

"I already asked her if she would give you the second ticket, and she said no. Her new boyfriend has a bong that Ken Kesey once touched and he's bringing that."

"A what?" I clarified.

"Just touched it. Didn't even put his mouth on it, just a hand. He *passed* it to someone," she told me.

After a long pause, I could only think of one thing to say.

"I'm going to take an Ambien, eat a box of sugar-free Oreos, and gas myself to death internally," I said before hanging up.

Ariane, in an effort to be a good friend and cheer me up, tried to get some tickets on craigslist, but the current asking price was two hundred dollars. Apiece. I hadn't even paid that much for the poster.

"What do you think?" she asked.

I waited for a second to let an Oreo gas bubble pass and then I let it all out.

"You know what? It's a scam. It is such a con! She's bringing a frog and people are selling their tickets for profit when

I have Nazi plunder sitting in my living room just waiting to be uncovered? Where is quality control on *Antiques Roadshow*? They get what they deserve, a bunch of wooden frogs and bongs. Scoundrels! Thugs! Crooks! What a bunch of sharks, getting our hopes all riled up and then turning around and giving tickets to people who couldn't even sell this stuff on eBay! I even do a really good impression of the old lady on the *Antiques Roadshow* commercial guessing the value of the Indian blanket. 'Six-fif-*tay*! Six-fif-*tay*!'"

"I'm really sorry," my friend said, trying to console me. "I know how much this meant to you."

"I don't even want to go on that stupid show now," I replied. "Even if they gave me tickets today. I hope they get nothing *but* frogs and bongs. I hope it's one giant day of frogs and bongs on *Antiques Shit Show*! My poster is a star! I'm telling you that my Mucha is the one chance they had at a headliner *and* a new commercial! My Mucha is the new Indian blanket!"

"What?" Ariane asked.

"Six-fif-*tay*!" I yelled into the phone. "Six-fif-*tay*!"

The days and weeks passed. I tried not to give it any more thought. I really did. But on the day I knew everyone who had tickets was descending on the fairgrounds, my hate was a cinder just waiting to combust and blow up that allegedly celebrity-fondled bong right along with it.

"I hope they get nothing but geodes," I said to my husband as I walked through the living room. "I hope those *Antiques Roadshow* people get nothing but rocks and Cabbage Patch dolls and a bunch of spoons with the names of states on them. Oregon spoons. I hope they get eight hours' worth of Oregon spoons! Imposters! Grifters! Crooks!"

My husband said nothing.

"Old thermoses," I said on my way back through the living room. "Fill your time slot with old thermoses formerly filled with milk, *Antiques Roadshow*! And war medals! Pottery from seventh-grade art classes! Snow globes! You falsifiers! Cheaters! Varmints!"

For the record, I'm not really sure who I was calling varmints—the ticket people on *Antiques Roadshow* or the people with the bongs and the frogs. All I know is that I wanted them all to suffer for the fact that I didn't get tickets and *I had the best thing.* "Maligners! Sophists! Purloiners!"

"Give thesaurus.com a rest," my husband said, not looking up from his book.

"*Filchers,*" I whispered.

"I'd look up alternative meanings on that one if I were you," he advised.

"Miscreants," I hissed.

"You know, if that thing is real," he said, nodding toward the Mucha on the wall, "then *Antiques Roadshow* just did you a big favor. If it's an honest-to-God original poster, you couldn't have it hanging right there! You'd have to sell it or give it to a museum; it wouldn't be hanging right *there* in our living room. If you love it as much as you say you do, love it enough to let it be fake. Love it enough to let it stay right where it is so you can look at it every day."

He was right, I realized. That was the curse of *Antiques Roadshow;* there was no winning either way. If your stuff was worthless, even if you loved it, you now knew it was crap. If it was valuable, chances were it was going to become someone else's valuable. How many people do you know who would keep an Indian blanket hanging over their couch if it was worth half a million dollars (not six-fif-*tay*)?

Would I sell my Mucha for half a million dollars? Absolutely. Did I want to? No.

So when Ariane called me the next day and told me not to look at the Sunday newspaper, I nodded and went ahead and did it.

"Eugene Show Stop Uncovers Rich Find," the headline read, and went on to report that a lost Norman Rockwell painting had been discovered at the fairgrounds the day before on *Antiques Roadshow.* Worth half a million dollars.

I saw it hanging at the museum the next time I was there, and the security guard standing next to the painting pointed to me and said, "Can you believe it? *Antiques Roadshow!*"

Either way, win or lose, you give up something.

Several months later, I found a new listing on Google for the Mucha Foundation. After I heard the tinkling of the theme song for *Antiques Roadshow* on the television, I thought I'd show them what for and e-mailed Marcus Mucha, the artist's grandson, with a letter and some pictures.

It was, he assured me, going to hang on my wall forever.

It was a fake.

Initially, I didn't believe it and stuck to my guns that the poster was such a unique piece that even the Mucha Foundation had no idea about it. In a way, a small part of me still believes that, although a larger part of me is delighted that when it's my husband's turn to pick out a TV show during our joint quality time, I have something better to look at than *Battlestar Galactica*.

At least the bong was a bust, too—I don't think it would have been worth anything unless it could have been DNA-traced to Ronald Reagan; the frog, however, was worth fifteen hundred dollars. Supposedly.

Doesn't matter. Right now, I'm waiting for a day in May when I find out whether I got tickets to *Antiques Roadshow* in Seattle.

I wonder what twelve new old stock antique mugs are worth.

THAT DAMN HOBO

*H*oly shit, there's a body in there!" my husband said as he looked at me with wide eyes and backed away from the bushes he had been poking at a moment ago.

I shook my head, closed my eyes, and yelled loud enough for all of our neighbors to hear: "You know what? *I hate the yoga people!* I hate them! This is all their fault!"

I was enraged. It *was* all their fault. There happened to be a yoga studio situated behind our house, and apparently, the hedges that lined the back portion of my yard and my neighbors' became something of an inconvenience to the people who decided to start using our alley as a shortcut into the yoga parking lot. And I was certain to a reasonably certain degree that some aloof and flexible jerkess who could dial an iPhone with a pedicured pinky toe from wheel pose had reported everyone on my side of the street to the city, because we all received warning letters of complaint. And they wanted the problem addressed.

Our slightly unruly hedges became such a problem for these uptight ladies, who really should just stay home and take Ativan instead of bringing their toxic energy to my street, that I came home one day to find large pink signs staked in the front yards of the neighbors on either side of me. The signs declared their property was a "public nuisance"—which is ridiculous, because either of these homes could be used as a movie set, they were so well tended. I don't know how I escaped the public staking, but I couldn't help feeling a little left out.

If the bushes were a little overgrown and a branch had the yearning to reach out and scratch a Range Rover driven by a woman in a tank top and jeggings, I didn't know, but I sure would've laughed if I'd seen it with my own eyes. The alley is not someplace that we wander freely, mainly because it is not territory that belongs to us. It is hobo turf, and as someone who'd rather not have to get a gun safe and stock up on rounds, I'd rather not go out there. Once you step past the back gate and into the hinterlands, it's like stepping into Narnia, but one that smells like urine and constantly has the clanging of glass bottles knocking together as they jostle about in a freshly stolen Safeway shopping cart, which I have since learned is the native call of the hobo.

I'd like to mention here that some people have insisted to me that "hobo" is an impolite term, and that I should use something a little more politically correct, like "residentially challenged" or "free-range tenant." But frankly, I don't see a problem with the word "hobo," nor do I understand why some people believe it to be derogatory. I believe "hobo" to have a genteel, jaunty connotation to it; I believe it to be a jocular reference to someone who might have fallen on hard times but is making the very best go of it.

Hobos like Tom Joad, they ride the rails, eat beans out of a can like I did in my early twenties. Hobos are friends with Woody Guthrie. Hobos carve tiny secret messages for other hobos on fence posts along the road. If I had my druthers, I would much prefer to picture my hobo humming to himself, happy all the time, carrying around his stuff in a bandana on a stick and taking a sip from a flask every now and then, than to open my eyes to the fact that a residentially challenged squatter is shooting up methamphetamine in between his toes roughly thirty feet from my back door.

All of the neighbors knew we had something of a diverse population in our alley due to our proximity to downtown and to a Safeway, a hub for cashing in bottles and cans for five cents apiece. Due to their serve-yourself soup bar, Safeway also became the hobo restaurant of choice, and that was evident by the number of folks with bits of grass stuck to the backs of their flannel shirts gulping down cups of minestrone under the cover of Pepperidge Farm end caps. As a result, I will eat foodstuffs shipped directly from China before I eat anything from that store that hasn't been hermetically sealed by a machine—and that's not elitist. That's just called being averse to open sores on or about the mouth area. I don't have them now. I don't want them later because I defied the odds and carelessly dove into a vat of Tuscan Tomato Herpes Bisque.

Still, eat your soup, rummage through my garbage, use my alley as a hobo highway; I didn't particularly care. You're a hobo. Even the day that I went searching in the back hedge for my dog's ball and found something quite different didn't really upset me all that much. There, tucked into an open space in between branches, was basically a hobo RV—a piece of cardboard, a Little Caesars pizza box, and a bag of empty soda cans that were undoubtedly headed for return at Safeway, followed by a bacchanalian chicken noodle feast.

You know what I did? Nothing. I left the stuff there. I figured that if the hobo needed a place to store his stuff, I was okay with it. However, I did feel a bit unsettled after I informed my neighbors of the discovery and learned that one of them had found used hypodermic needles in her kid's playhouse, and the other had suspicions that the temporary required-by-construction port-o-potty in her backyard might have been an attraction of sorts.

But I still let my hobo use my bushes as a master bedroom closet.

Then came the day a year later when I noticed something odd in my garlic bed. There were "deposits" in uncouth places. True, I have a little dog. She is a very weird, particular sort of creature that has meticulous habits, and that includes where she conducts private time. To tell the truth, she takes her private time so seriously that I have no idea where she goes unless we're on a walk, and then she'll go in front of people who are standing in their front yard. I know she wasn't the one who made dirty in the garlic bed. In a self-defense mechanism, I cleaned up the deposits and convinced myself that my dog was simply acting out of character, even though I found the curiosities in the exact spot where a full-size human would squat over the garden border.

My neighbor's port-o-potty, by the way, had been removed when construction on her house had been completed a month before. Regardless, I put a lock on the back gate and I moved on.

The following week, after seven days of rain and freezing temperatures, I discovered a structure of sorts under my back gate, bridging the muddy span between the alley and the backyard for easy, unencumbered passage, consisting of boards probably ripped off my neighbor's fence. It was work unfettered by details and constructed by someone who subsisted on a strict diet of soup. I looked at my dog. I knew she didn't build it. Her eyes told me she wasn't the garlic pooper, either.

The week after that, my little dog woke me up at 6:30 a.m. to alert me that something was amiss at our front door. After I stumbled down the stairs, I found a man I had never seen before standing in front of my neighbor's house, who turned and ambled across the street with the speed of a threatened silverback as soon as I opened the door. Within three seconds, he was quickly on my porch as clouds of frost shot out of his mouth and he waved his arms boldly about.

"I need gas!" he demanded, his eyes bulging. "I need lawn mower gas right now! How much do you have? I'm going to the Four Corners!"

"We don't have a lawn mower!" I replied quickly, which was equally insane because he should have known that. There was no doubt in my mind that he'd been in our backyard. Plus, a hobo doesn't go very far without his stuff, maybe a block or two, so that meant that his base camp was nearby. Very nearby.

Aside from that, I would never give a hobo gas, even if I did want him to relocate to another state. In Phoenix, a hobo arsonist tried to set our backyard on fire in the middle of the night and there I was when the fire department arrived, holding a hose and wearing just a tank top and a pair of Fruit of the Loom white cotton briefs. You only need to make that mistake once.

I shut the door quickly and couldn't help being disappointed. He didn't have a bandana on a stick, he wasn't humming, and he did not seem jolly in the least. My hobo was mean. And high. He was just a crackhead, one who'd become unaccustomed to using toilet paper and really would drive a lawn mower to the border of Arizona and Utah if the voices demanded it.

That was the last time I encountered the hobo or any sign of him, except when I saw him at Safeway several months later, pushing a stolen grocery cart full of stuff, including a lampshade I thought I could really do something with. Clearly, his dreams of reaching the Four Corners on a lawn mower had not been realized, and he had replaced that reverie with spitting at traffic instead.

Then the complaint letter arrived, giving us ten days to maintain the bushes in the alley or face a fine from the city. We bought a pole trimmer, unlocked the back gate, noticed the bridge was gone—clearly if you lock out a hobo, he takes back his gifts—and crossed the border into hobo Narnia.

We were halfway done when my husband shut off the trimmer.

"What's in there?" he asked, pointing hesitantly to the portion of the bushes he had just cut.

There was a large mass of something blue, several bags of empty soda cans, and a pair of jeans.

"That's the hobo's apartment," I said nervously, shooting a glance down the alley in case he was on his way home, even though I knew I'd hear the clatter of beer bottles long before he rounded the corner and the spitting started.

"There's something in there," my husband said, leaning in closer. "Holy shit! There's a body in there!"

Now, I suppose it would be different if this were the first body my husband had suddenly found this year, but it wasn't (although I'm not allowed to write about it because it's "still not funny, Laurie"; I just checked). The thought of a deceased free-range hobo filled me with dread, fear, and, most of all, anger. I couldn't believe this was about to happen again. After the last body (still not funny; I checked again) it took two weeks of watching the entire catalog of Pixar movies and eating Domino's Pizza every night before my husband had calmed down enough to resist poking me every time I closed my eyes.

This was really unfair. I didn't want him to go through the trauma of finding a second dead person within a square mile, and personally, I can only watch *Cars 2* once a year. If the yoga people didn't insist on using the alley as their own personal street and then feel they had the right to complain to the city that our bushes were scratching their cars, we wouldn't be back here in the first place. The last thing I ever want to do on any day is find a dead hobo, because once you discover one, you can't undiscover it.

I felt terrible that I did not give him gas that day. And I'm sorry he died alone. But at least he made it back to his apartment. Clearly, he went peacefully in the comfort of his own nest, resting on a bed of leaves and surrounded by the roughly thirty-eight balls he had likely stolen from my dog.

I obviously couldn't live with the thought of a dying hobo haunting my backyard. I had predecided the minute I spotted him lying there that our house would be up for sale by sundown.

My anger turned to rage when I heard the crunch of gravel under tires and I knew there was a yoga person turning into the parking lot. I wouldn't be out here if it weren't for them and their complaining. If it weren't for them, the hobo could have been found by a subsequent homeowner who thought that grooming the back of his house was just as important as grooming the front, or by some little kids poking around in places they shouldn't have been poking.

"You know what?" I yelled loud enough for all of our neighbors to hear me. "*I hate the yoga people!* I hate them! This is all their fault!"

"I agree. I hate them, too. Now help me," my husband said as he reached toward the mound, and with gloved hands, we each pulled the bundle of blue out. It wasn't heavy, but then again, it's not like you can't stick a mummy in a backpack and hike out of a tomb with it.

I shuddered. The wave of anxiety swallowing my insides grew larger when we pulled what turned out to be a filthy blue comforter out of the bushes. Under it, I saw the outline of a body on its side, bent at the knees and one arm under the head.

I took a deep breath. "How do we do this?" I asked my husband, since he was the one with the experience. We pulled the comforter back at the same time, expecting to see our hobo, now done in leather.

But there was nothing. Just leaves. Lots of leaves and dirt. The comforter was empty. No body. No dead hobo. No *Ratatouille* and a large Meat Lovers on the menu for tonight. The tragedy that was getting ready to swallow our lives or at least the rest of the afternoon had been undone.

The hobo lived. Probably, maybe. Well, perhaps the hobo lived, and that was good enough for me as long as he wasn't dead within my property lines.

We simply looked at each other as we dropped our respective corners and exhaled huge sighs of relief. From behind me, I heard another set of tires on gravel, then a short honk of a car horn. I turned to see a Volvo, a nice, new, shiny Volvo, stopped and waiting for us to get out of the way. I waved slightly, and as the driver drove slowly past toward the parking lot of the yoga studio, she waved back.

"Sor-ree!" She grinned with a huge white smile. "I need to get to class."

"No problem," I said as I smiled back. "We were completely and utterly in your way as a driver who has co-opted our alley."

"Is that your house right there?" the yoga person said as she pointed to my backyard, and I got ready for a lecture about how errant laurel branches can decimate the Blue Book value of a Volvo that she just drove off a car lot yesterday.

"Yep," I said, getting my pointer finger ready for an alley screaming match. It was all about to go down, hobo style.

"I don't want you to think that I'm spying," she said with a laugh, which disarmed me. "But as I drive by I can see your yard through the bushes, and your garden looks so beautiful. Everything is so green and healthy!"

"Well, I wouldn't say it was organic, but we did have a special kind of fertilizer," I said as I smiled back, then quickly added, "Hey! Would you like some homegrown garlic?"

THE POTTY MOUTH AT THE TABLE

I couldn't believe it. I had just been bitch slapped.

I sat there stunned for seconds afterward in the eerie quiet that followed. I looked out at the lecture hall filled with students as sixty pairs of eyes turned toward me, the silence invading the room like barefooted Huns. As soon as I recovered my senses, I looked down the table of panelists and at the tiny man in the stupid fedora who had just insulted me publicly and continued right on with his nasal diatribe.

I had never met this man before; our first meeting had been fifteen minutes earlier when we were introduced by the moderator of a writing panel, Humor in Literature. We'd both been invited to speak at this writing conference, and while I am not a scholar of poetry, I am a pretty good judge of character when it comes to tiny, assholian men who fancy fedora hats. And when I read his bio in the conference booklet—all instructors were asked to write their own bios—my suspicions were confirmed. He wrote that he considered himself to be one of the most admired, acknowledged, and humorous poets of this day and age. And by age, I mean the age of bipedal mankind.

He was cordial but abrupt when we were introduced; not friendly, not rude, just curt, which was fine by me—I certainly wasn't expecting a hug. Some people don't do well in social situations; writers are notorious for this, and I wasn't going on a date with the guy, nor were we scheduled to cage fight, so why the attitude, Mr. Poet? Hey, it's fine by me: Don't say anything back or look me in the eye when I said it was nice to meet you. Especially when we will be doing a reading together on the last night of the conference and will have to see each other again—that won't be awkward at all.

I had no further contact with Mr. Poet after that crusty exchange. When the panel began, we were asked to introduce ourselves and say a little something about our background to the class, which was so full that there were people standing in the back, leaning against the walls. The first writer on the dais talked about the memoir she wrote and how she prepared for it. Everyone was very responsive, and when it came my turn to speak I said that I loved writing humor because every time I showed my underwear to a stranger by accident, or tossed a naked tampon out of my purse at a bag boy, talking and laughing about it made it feel less shitty.

The audience laughed and I settled into my seat, a little more comfortable now that introductions had been made. Except for Mr. Poet, who stood up, introduced himself, mentioned the award that his latest poem had won, and proceeded to say, "You can tell when a person truly understands what humor is when they do not have to resort to profanity, unlike the potty mouth at the table." With that, he threw me a look of disdain so pure and disgusted, it was followed by the exclamation point of snotty expressions, the exaggerated eye roll.

The room flatlined as every eye in it immediately glided down the table to me, the offender—the Potty Mouth. I'm sure my jaw was caught in a free fall before I pretended it was funny, but it was no use. It was out there; the diss was as blatant and direct as one baby mama to another with kids the exact same age—and with the exact same noses—standing in line at the Dollar Store, buying diapers.

I decided not to respond to Mr. Poet's comment, even though I was so embarrassed that I don't know how my ears didn't light my neighbors on fire. I was stunned, and the embarrassment was so overwhelming that for a moment I felt dizzy.

Would I have liked to reach over and give him one of my mother's "I don't think you'll be doing that again" pinches, flesh vise-gripped so effectively that it would leave physical and emotional scars for decades? Yes, yes, I would have liked that very much. But there was no way I was going to stoop to his level. People had attended this panel to hear writers talk about humor, not to watch a slap fight between two assholes, one in a hat (and it's definitely an Asshole Fight if any participant is wearing a hat).

Let it be known, however, that due to the fact that I have two younger sisters close in age, I am *very* versed in the art of parking lot fights, especially the kicking aspect, and I am more than willing to bring those skills indoors, *my friend.*

He, however, went on to recite his entire poem word for word, and I happen to know this for a fact because he printed out five pages of it and handed them out to everyone who passed by one of the classroom windows.

My outward politeness, however, did not stop me from thinking of a thousand retorts in my head:

"Who are you, Columbo? Take off your friggin' hat already; it's a hundred and fifteen degrees outside and the runway at the airport just melted. Get an all-season identifier, like a birthmark or a monocle."

"I want to peel the skin off your head like a grape. There's certainly enough hot air under that fedora to steam your bald head, you talking onion."

"I googled you after I read your stupid bio. You can tell when a writer truly understands humor when he doesn't have to write about oral sex and wieners in every single shitty poem to get a laugh. *Yes. I said shitty. Again. Shitty shitty shitty*."

I thought of all those things and more.

I just didn't say them.

My ears were still a little hot by the time the class ended two hours later, but I was comforted when several students came up afterward and said nice things to me. I decided to chalk the experience up to lack of social skills on his part because he was probably such an ugly baby that no one would hold him; and I wouldn't rule out Tourette's or a crest in a manic cycle that had yet to be addressed.

So I went about my business during the conference, meeting nice people and having a good time, until I was headed back to my hotel the next day. Who was coming toward me but Mr. Oral Sex Poet. There was no way to blend into a crowd; there were just two of us on the path. I knew it was him. He was still wearing his hat.

Now, just to be clear, I am not the nicest person in the world, and I have never pretended to be. However, I knew

I had two options here: smile and say hello or knock off his hat with a "Mom said to stop touching me" kick and go for the back of his neck where the flesh was the loosest to get the best grip for the de-gloving. (See? I can be not nice, too.)

But as we got closer, I hoped that maybe I had made a mistake; maybe he did mean the comment to be funny but just delivered it wrong, or just ended up saying something he didn't truly intend. He was a couple of yards away from me when I smiled and made myself say "Hi," not sarcastically, not snottily, but pleasantly. It was, I have to say, almost a cheerful greeting. As if to say: Let's wipe the slate clean, Mr. Oral Sex Poet. Because after all, I decided, what kind of adult man calls an adult woman a Potty Mouth in front of sixty other adults and means it?

The same kind of man, apparently, who sees a Potty Mouth waving and saying hello to him on an otherwise deserted sidewalk—then sneers and literally turns his nose up.

Well, I thought, my hand still in the air midwave. *Well.*

I guess he showed me.

Didn't he?

The last night of the conference, I arrived at the hall where the reading was about to take place and checked in with the coordinator to see whether there were any last-minute things I should know about.

"You're scheduled to read first," she informed me, and that I was to be followed by Mr. Oral Sex Poet, whom I was decidedly not going to wave to this time. "We're taping this, so if you'd like a copy, let me know. The poet after you is submitting this video to an award panel, and as long as I'm making one copy, I can make another. My battery can last an hour, so you'll be fine on time."

It was a great reading. I had a wonderful time. The audience was awesome, all except for the wrinkled woman in the front row who shook her head adamantly when I asked whether they wanted to hear another piece and she cheered for the poet instead. I saw you, lady. I saw you. But I didn't cast one glance in her direction, nor did I look at Mr. Oral Sex Poet, who still sat with his hat on, as I read piece after piece, occasionally eyeing the video camera until the green light switched to red and the battery power was nearly spent.

Kicked, I thought to myself as I turned my head and looked straight at him, smiling cheerfully.

Consider your ass very much kicked.

That's right, my friend. I said *ass.*

DON'T MAKE ME THE ASSHOLE

I knew it.

I. Knew. It.

The trap I had set only yesterday had been sprung, and the proof was right there before my eyes. My bath puff, green, unraveled, and springy, was in the second tier of the bath caddy that hung down from the neck of the showerhead.

And that was not where I had left it.

I pursed my lips together and shook my head.

Roughly twenty-four hours before, I suspected something was amiss. For days now, even possibly weeks, I had a feeling the puff was not where I had left it. Its position would be slightly askew, barely noticeable to the naked eye, but I could tell that my puff had been tampered with. I dismissed the notion, sure that I was wrong. I had to be wrong. Who would use another person's puff? Intentionally? It's the equivalent of using someone else's toothbrush or hairbrush, or used chewing gum plucked off the underside of a table.

Who moved my puff? Who would even touch my puff? You couldn't *pay* me to touch a strange puff; even looking at other people's used puffs made me feel queasy. Now I couldn't even bring myself to look at my own puff. I put on rubber gloves and plucked it out of the shower caddy with a pair of salad tongs and tossed it unceremoniously into the trash bin.

That's when it dawned on me—*the call was coming from inside the house*. There were only two possible suspects: my husband and our nineteen-year-old nephew, Derek, who was staying with us for the summer.

Obviously, my husband would respect the sanctity of the puff. It is very clear in my house that I am Anti-Cootie. He knows all too well that I won't even take a sip from a glass someone else has mouthed as a result of letting my then three-year-old nephew, Nicholas, take a "sip" from my glass of water, only to return it to me looking like a Chicken McNugget smoothie.

So that left only one possibility. A flash of horror gripped my bones and I had to resist the urge to cry out loud, although my mouth still made the movements.

"Oh my God, oh my God," I whispered, thinking, *Why, why, why would a young man go into a shower and start touching unfamiliar puffs?* Especially one that was frayed and collapsing—it was clear, that was no young puff. It had miles on it, having already scratched and clawed its way through life, and now it lay used and feeble on the second shelf. I had to bunch it up to even make it workable. And now, it was soiled and shameful in a pitiful netted heap, used by others without protesting a bit.

Dirty puff. Dirty, dirty puff. I wasn't sure from which perspective I should throw up first—mine or my nephew's.

As I washed without the puff for the first time in ages, knowing I was not getting clean with soap alone, I took some small comfort in knowing I was not smearing questionable DNA all over my body. As I stood under the stream of water with my eyes closed and suds pooling around my ankles, one thing was clear: I was going to have to broach the situation and put an end to the sharing of the puff.

I didn't want to blurt it out and risk embarrassing my nephew. I felt a grand approach was much better than an appointed one; after all, mysteries of the body and accompanying long stares are far more comfortable to deal with when they are left on a somewhat ambiguous note. I considered leaving a note saying, "Dear People Living in My House: I don't mean to be selfish, but the puff in the shower is not community property. It belongs to the Lady. Who will now be getting a new one. With her name on it," on the bathroom mirror in a swirly, cheeky font, but I decided on another, underhanded, more passive-aggressive route.

And then, when I was dressed, I got my car keys.

When I returned, the two gentlemen I resided with were sharing a bag of Fritos and a can of bean dip, which, by the way, I purchased because it's my Signature Snack, which they had raided from the Lady's Private Snack Closet. My husband stopped chewing and tried to hide a gargantuan portion of refried beans under his tongue when I walked through the door.

"I'm calling a family meeting," I announced.

"Ellbuoyoomoooh," he said.

"Yes, you will buy me more, but that is not the objective of this family meeting. Something kooky is happening in the shower," I said, opening the bag I'd returned home with.

My husband gulped several Fritos whole like a snake. "It all goes down the drain," he protested.

"*That* is an urban myth," I replied, letting go of the bag. "If I stuck a black light in there, I bet it would light up like a Broadway marquee. *It does not all go down the drain.* The world is not your urinal. And I have a situation that is possibly more urgent than even that."

No one said a word.

"For the last several days, I have noticed that my puff is not in the same place where I left it," I explained slowly. "So I feel it necessary to explain that a bath puff is a single-user sort of thing. Like a hairbrush. Or a retainer. Or—"

"Don't say 'tampon' in front of Derek," my husband said as he cupped a hand to the side of his mouth to block Derek's view, and then mouthed, "He's just a boy."

"I wasn't going to say that," I said, shaking my head.

"I thought you were," my husband replied.

"No, I wasn't going to," I insisted.

"Are you sure?" he asked. "Because it looked like you were going to say something . . . like that."

My mouth started moving because I had so much to say but no words came out.

"I was going to say dental floss!" I finally asserted. "*Dental floss.* And keep your hands off my goddamn frigging bean dip! It's my Signature Snack. *You know that.*"

"Are you making dinner soon?" Derek asked. "What are we having?"

I took a deep breath and then spit out, "I want to talk about bath puffs. I want to talk about someone touching something that's mine and private and should remain mine and private. No one should be touching my puff, do you understand? No one touches my puff. No one. But *me.* I am the only one who has touching privileges over my puff."

The air was still in the room for a moment.

"But," my husband began. "We're married. I thought we were . . . *one.*"

The air went still in the next moment.

"What?" I questioned. "No. *No.* We are not *one.* Who told you we were one? Because. No, we are not one. You are one. I am two. Or I am one and you are two. It doesn't matter, but we can't both be one."

My husband didn't say a word.

I pointed at him. "*Uno,*" I said very clearly, then pointed to myself, "and *dos. Uno* and *dos.* Don't say anything, Derek."

"I would never touch your puff," he said anyway, and that's when I wanted to light myself on fire.

"Don't say another word, Derek." I turned back to my husband: "Why are you puff touching? Why? How long have we had a community puff when only one person in the community knew?"

"I don't know," my husband said, shaking his head. "We got married in 1996, so . . ." And then he started counting on his fingers.

"Oh my God. *Oh my God.*" My hands flew to the sides of my head. "You are shitting me. *Shitting me.* I am going to pass out. I want to pass out. What is going on here? Is my sister my mom, too?!"

"I thought you were the oldest," Derek said.

"Not the point, honey," I yelled at my nephew. "Not the point. It's a metaphor!"

"It's actually not a metaphor; it's an analogy," my husband corrected.

"*Shut up,*" I demanded. "You still have student loans!"

I reached back into the bag and pulled out a long plastic tube with rainbow colors inside and ripped it open.

"You are green!" I said as I threw a brand-new bath puff at Derek. "I am pink! And Mr. One is purple!"

Then I had to lay down the Laws of the Bath Puff, which I augmented with hand motions simply to avoid any confusion. They are as follows:

1. Just because we sit on the same potty does not mean it's okay to put *my* puff on your butt.

2. I *never* want to stand in the shower again and say to myself, "Is that . . . mine?"

3. If you forget your puff color, you surrender your right to use a puff, *any* puff, during that period in which ownership is unclear until you have reconfirmed your assigned hue.

4. The moment the puff leaves the tub/shower area, it is not allowed in any other part of the house that is not the trash.

5. We should make a concerted effort to never let our individual puffs graze, brush against, or have any physical contact with one another.

6. And I really don't want anyone else touching my soap when he is naked, either.

7. Don't make me the asshole. Because you are making me an asshole for calling you out for violating unspoken but generally understood Cootie Code.

Of course, I am living with two males, whose response to the laying of the law was:

"Puff off."

"Puff you."

"Shut the puff up."

"Never leave a puff behind."

"I'm going to put my puff on the knob."

And if they think that's funny, fine. Then that's funny. As long as we have our own netted globes teeming with DNA to scrub the dead skin cells off our own bodies, they can laugh all they want. They *should* laugh. Laugh it up. Ha-ha-ha-ha-ha. How funny!

It's not going to be so funny, though, when they see a note on the Lady's Private Snack Closet addressing some missing savory items, particularly bean dip, printed in the boldest font she could possibly find.

LEGENDS OF THE FALL

MIDDAY.

THE LIGHT ON A PHONE RESTING ON A HALL TABLE
SIGNALS RED AS IT RINGS.

THE VOICE OF A WOMAN CALLS OUT.

> **LAURIE** (Voice-over)
> I got it, hon!

A HAND PICKS IT UP. IT BELONGS TO **LAURIE**
(INDETERMINATE AGE, CURLY HAIR, MOST OF THE LEFT
SIDE IN A PONYTAIL, MOST OF THE RIGHT HALF TUCKED
BEHIND HER EAR, WEARING A BROWN VELOUR HOODIE—
CLEARLY HER PAJAMAS. SHE'S CHEWING ON A FIBER BAR AS
SHE PICKS UP THE PHONE, HER MOUTH SMACKING LOUDLY
BECAUSE THERE IS NO ONE ELSE IN THE HOUSE TO YELL AT
HER.)

LAURIE (CONT'D)

Hello?

CUT TO A KITCHEN IN A LARGE TRACT HOME WITH COUNTERS FILLED WITH EVERY SMALL ELECTRICAL APPLIANCE EVER INVENTED AND SOLD, INCLUDING TWO MICROWAVES, A CONVECTION OVEN, A BLENDER, TWO COFFEEMAKERS. CROCKS FILLED WITH DECORATIVE SPATULAS ARE CRAMMED IN BETWEEN, AS ARE FLAMELESS CANDLES AND BLOCKS OF COLORFUL SILICONE KNIVES. SEVERAL BOXES MARKED "QVC" ON THE SIDES ARE OPENED AND VISIBLE IN THE BACKGROUND. **MOM**, A WOMAN BEARING A STRIKING RESEMBLANCE TO **LAURIE**, PLUS TWENTY-TWO YEARS, HAS A CORDLESS PHONE IN HER HAND. SHE IS CHEWING ON A COOKIE AND IS WEARING A BROWN VELOUR HOODIE. THERE IS A PACKING PEANUT IN HER HAIR.

CUT BACK TO **LAURIE**. A SMALL CHUNK OF FIBER BAR TUMBLES OUT OF HER MOUTH. SHE KEEPS CHEWING.

LAURIE

Hey, mom. What's—

CUT TO **MOM**.

MOM

Yeah, listen. I don't know
if anyone told you, but uh, we were
at the hospital Thursday.

CUT TO **LAURIE**.

LAURIE

Oh my God. What happened?

CUT TO **MOM**.

MOM

Oh, God. It's your sister.

LAURIE

Oh, no! Lisa?

MOM

Your sister!

LAURIE

Lisa?

MOM

The one closest to you.

CUT TO **LAURIE**.

LAURIE

I said "Lisa?"

MOM

In age.

LAURIE

Oh, Linda.

CUT TO **MOM**.

MOM

So your sister was just in the hospital.

LAURIE

Lisa?

MOM

Have you been drinking? I'm not
playing games with you. Are
you ready for me to tell
you about your sister's tragedy?
or are you going to play games?

CUT TO **LAURIE**.

LAURIE

I'm ready. I'm actually very excited.

LAURIE WALKS INTO THE BATHROOM AND SHUTS THE DOOR.

CUT TO **MOM**.

SHE BITES INTO ANOTHER COOKIE. A PIECE OF IT FALLS OUT OF HER MOUTH.

> **MOM**
> Fine. She was at school, you know she's
> teaching there, when she opened
> a Diet Pepsi while the kids were at recess.

CUT TO BATHROOM DOOR. SILENCE.

CUT TO **MOM**.

> **MOM** (CONT'D)
> Are you listening to me? This
> is a very important part of the story.

> **LAURIE** (THROUGH PHONE)
> I'm all ears.

FLASHBACK: CUT TO **LINDA**, A SUBURBAN VERSION OF **LAURIE**, WITH BLONDE HAIR, MANICURED FINGERNAILS, PERFECT MAKEUP, SITTING AT HER DESK IN A CLASSROOM AND WEARING A PINK VELOUR HOODIE. SHE OPENS THE DIET PEPSI.

LAURIE NOTARO

> **MOM** (V.O.)
> Usually, she says she gets a
> glass of ice with her Diet
> Pepsi, but this time, she didn't.
> I don't know why. She just didn't.

LINDA LOOKS AT THE CAN, STICKING ONE MANICURED
FINGER IN IT AND SUDDENLY PULLING IT BACK OUT, AS IF
THE SODA WERE BOILING WATER. THEN SHE SHRUGS AND
POLISHES OFF THE HOT CAN OF SODA IN A MATTER OF GULPS.

> **MOM** (V.O.)
> She drank it very fast, and
> all of the bubbles went
> to her chest! But she said
> the pain was so big in her chest
> that she had to hold
> her breath! The pain, the pain!

LINDA'S EYES GET WIDE. IT ALL GOES BLACK. ONE SECOND.
TWO SECONDS. THREE SECONDS.

CUT TO A BLURRY VISION OF SOMETHING GRAY, WHICH
COMES INTO FOCUS AS A TEXTILE. FROM THE RIGHT
CORNER, SOMETHING DARK SPREADS QUICKLY INTO THE
FRAME. AN AUDIBLE, SMALL HISS OF CARBONATION IS
HEARD.

MOM (V.O.)
Then, the next thing you
know, she woke up and she
was looking at carpet. She
had no idea where she was.
Finally, she came to and
realized she'd fainted.

CLOSE-UP OF **LINDA**'S EYES DARTING BACK AND FORTH.
PANIC. PANIC. THE FAINT SOUNDS OF CHILDREN'S LAUGHTER
ECHO IN THE BACKGROUND. A SPARROW WHISTLES.

THE SHOT GETS SHAKY AS SCOPE OF THE CLASSROOM IS
QUICKLY TAKEN IN, A CUT TO THE LEFT AND A CUT TO THE
RIGHT. THE ANGLE GAINS HEIGHT, DIPS A LITTLE, THEN
SIMPLY CUTS WILDLY ABOUT.

SHOT OF A FAT MAN IN A TIE LOOKING DOWN. A
NONDESCRIPT MIDDLE-AGED WOMAN JOINS HIM.
AND ANOTHER. AND ANOTHER. THE JANITOR STANDS
THERE WITH A MOP IN HIS HANDS. A CROWD OF **LINDA**'S
COWORKERS FORMS.

MOM (V.O.)
She got herself to the phone
and called her principal,
who came over right away.

NONDESCRIPT MIDDLE-AGED WOMAN

(BENDING OVER AND TALKING LOUDLY)

Linda, what is your husband's phone number?

LINDA (V.O.)

I-I-I don't know. Are you angels?

Why am I not looking down

on my body? Is it because

Safeway gave me too much

change and I didn't say

anything? But I watch Lifetime

TV for women. That's like

extra credit for heaven.

CUT TO **MOM**, WHERE AN ANGRY **LINDA** WALKS INTO THE
SHOT (WEARING PINK HOODIE) AND GRABS THE PHONE
OUT OF **MOM**'S HAND.

LINDA (V.O., CONT'D)

I did *not* say that. Mom has her

facts all wrong. And it wasn't

a Diet Pepsi. It was a Diet Vanilla Coke!

CUT TO BATHROOM DOOR.

LAURIE

So Diet Vanilla Coke attacked

You? Not diet pepsi?

MOM'S KITCHEN: CUT TO **LINDA**.

LINDA

Yes. And you should know
that I never let go of the Diet
Vanilla Coke. I held on to it
the whole time.

CUT TO CLASSROOM: A HAND WITH MANICURED
FINGERNAILS GRASPING A CAN OF DIET VANILLA COKE,
FALLING FORWARD IN VERY SLOW MOTION.

CUT TO BATHROOM DOOR.

LAURIE

What do you mean? What
happened to it? Did it land upright?

CUT TO CLASSROOM: THE CAN, STILL WITH THE HAND
CLUTCHING IT (SLO-MO), COMES IN BRUTAL CONTACT WITH
THE GRAY CARPET WITH AN ECHOING *THUD!* SODA SPLASHES
UP AND OUT OF THE MOUTH HOLE, LIKE A TSUNAMI.

LINDA (V.O.)

Well, not really. Most of it sprayed
all over my students' desks.

CLOSE-UP ON DESK SURFACE. DROPS OF HISSING BROWN RAIN FALL RELENTLESSLY.

SILENCE AS THE CRACKLING OF THE SODA DIES OUT.

PULL BACK FROM THE CAN, AS IT IS NOW TIPPED ON ITS SIDE, LEAKING LIKE AN OIL RIG, PULL BACK, PULL BACK, UNTIL A STRAND OF BLONDE HAIR COMES INTO FRAME, THEN MORE STRANDS, THEN A HEAD, AS THE POOL OF SODA OVERTAKES AND RUSHES THROUGH THE BLONDE HAIR. FIZZLING IS HEARD.

> **LINDA** (V.O., CONT'D)
> But most of it soaked my hair. What is that clicking noise? Is that the phone? Do you think President Obama is listening to us?

CUT TO **LAURIE**, HOLDING HERSELF UP IN THE BATHROOM DOORWAY, LAUGHING SILENTLY WITH TEARS STREAMING DOWN HER FACE.

MOM'S KITCHEN: CUT TO **LINDA**, LOOKING INTO THE PHONE WITH ANNOYANCE.

> **LINDA**
> (THROUGH PHONE)
> Are you there?

CUT TO **LAURIE**, STILL PROPPED UP IN THE DOORWAY, STILL
SILENT, NODDING, THEN WIPING AWAY A TEAR.

> **LAURIE**
> Uh-huh.

> **LINDA** (THROUGH PHONE)
> Anyway, that wasn't the worst part.
> Before the paramedics wheeled me out—

CUT TO **LAURIE**, RAISING HER HAND.

> **LAURIE**
> Wait, wait—you called 911?

> **LINDA** (THROUGH PHONE)
> (HEAVY, DEEP SIGH)
> Someone thought I hit my head
> on the way down.

CUT TO CLASSROOM: **LINDA** LOOKS LIKE
A GULLIVER SMOOSHED INTO A TEENY-TINY DESK,
HER HEAD BACK, WHILE A NONDESCRIPT MIDDLE-AGED
WOMAN FANS HER WITH AN *OPRAH* MAGAZINE.
PRINCIPAL LOOKS ON.

NONDESCRIPT MIDDLE-AGED WOMAN

(PICKING UP A STRAND OF

LINDA'S DRIPPING HAIR)

We should call someone.

This isn't blood but it could be

plasma or brain water. She saw

angels! Linda, did you see the Virgin Mary?

PRINCIPAL

No, no, no. This is a Lutheran school.

No Virgin Mary talk. That

could affect our funding.

CUT TO **MOM**'S KITCHEN: **LINDA** IS EATING A COOKIE.

LINDA

So the worst part was that when the paramedics were

wheeling me out to go to the hospital so I could

get an EKG, a brain scan, and blood work done,

one of the paramedics—

BACK TO CLASSROOM: **LINDA** IS ON A STRETCHER. ALL

COWORKERS ARE GATHERED AROUND. SHE IS HOLDING

THE DIET VANILLA COKE CAN ON HER ABDOMEN. A

PARAMEDIC STANDS NEXT TO HER WITH A CLIPBOARD.

PARAMEDIC

Weight?

LINDA

(WITH EYES CLOSED)

That's okay, sir. I'm in no

hurry to hear that I'm

probably going to die today.

PARAMEDIC

No, I need your weight, ma'am.

Your weight.

(Pats his belly to emphasize)

ALL HEADS OF COWORKERS TURN TOWARD **LINDA**.

LINDA

Oh. My weight? Oh. Um. One hundred and, um . . .

(Whispers something inaudible)

CLOSE-UP OF NONDESCRIPT MIDDLE-AGED WOMAN.

NONDESCRIPT MIDDLE-AGED WOMAN

(SHAKES HER HEAD, LOOKS AT PRINCIPAL, MOUTHS,

WITH GREAT EXAGGERATION)

Lowball.

BACK TO **LAURIE**, STLL STANDING IN BATHROOM DOORWAY.

LAURIE

You told them? You told them
how much you weighed?

BACK TO **MOM**'S KITCHEN.

LINDA

He asked me! I had to!

BACK TO **LAURIE**, NOW IN KITCHEN, OPENING PANTRY.

LAURIE

No you didn't! You did not!
They're not the Gestapo! He
didn't know! Paramedics aren't
psychic weight guessers! You
were lying down! That takes
like forty pounds off right there!
You should know these things!

LINDA

I couldn't lie. I was in front of
my principal.

LAURIE

Your principal saw you lose
consciousness because you drank
a hot Diet Pepsi too fast!

LINDA

Diet Vanilla Coke.

LAURIE

Well, believe me, the moment soda
dripped on his shoes from your
head, respect was long gone.

CUT TO **LINDA**.

LINDA

That is not true. He makes sure I
have ice every day in my room now.

CUT TO **LAURIE**.

LAURIE

That's not respect. That's just
cheaper than being sued by the
parents of thirty kids who just watched
their thirsty teacher black out
after slamming a soda that she
left in her car for too long.

LINDA

It was only out there until lunch.

LAURIE

So, how are you?

BACK TO **MOM**'S KITCHEN: **MOM** IS LEANING OVER **LINDA**'S
SHOULDER.

MOM

(YELLING TOWARD THE PHONE)

Nothing was wrong. Can you believe
it? A brain X-ray, nothing was
wrong, they said. After all of
that. The doctors were stumped.
It's a medical mystery.

BACK TO.

LAURIE

Really? No one detected any drama?
Because I understand that
Linda theater is now in its forty-second season.

BACK TO **MOM**'S KITCHEN.

MOM

No, no trauma. There was no
trauma, was there, Lin?

LINDA

No. They would have kept me
there until dinnertime, as it was,
all I had that day was the
Diet Vanilla Coke. I didn't even get Jell-O.

MOM

They don't feed medical mystery patients.
It could upset the tests!

LAURIE

I can't believe that there's no test
for Diet Pepsi attacks.

LINDA

Well, from now on, I'm sticking to iced tea.

LAURIE

I'd watch it if I were you. A
reckless squeeze of a lemon
and before you know it,
everyone knows how much you weigh.

LOUD CLICK IS HEARD ON THE PHONE LINE.

LINDA

I heard that clicking noise again.

LAURIE

(WHISPERING)

It's President Obama!

MOM

(VERY LOUDLY)

I didn't vote for you!

I only vote for mavericks!

LAURIE

He already knows that, Mom.

He can hear you shouting through the TV.

MOM

I'm hanging up. I just wanted

to let you know that your sister was okay.

LAURIE

Why, did something happen to Lisa?

LINDA

(VOICE FADING AWAY)

Mom, I was going to eat that cookie!

No, we don't have the same

germs.

PHONE LINE GOES DEAD. A SUDDEN BOOM IS HEARD,

LIKE SOMEONE HAS JUST FALLEN DOWN THE STAIRS.

THE POTTY MOUTH AT THE TABLE

LAURIE RUNS INTO THE HALLWAY, WHERE HER HUSBAND IS SPRAWLED OUT ON THE FLOOR, APPARENTLY UNCONSCIOUS. ON HIS BELLY IS A CAN OF DIET PEPSI HE HOLDS IN ONE HAND; THE CIRCLE OF THE LOGO HAS BEEN MADE INTO A FACE, WITH THE EYES X'D OUT. ON HIS CHEST IS A NOTE WITH HIS HANDWRITING ON IT. IT SAYS, IN LARGE BLACK LETTERS, "NO ICE! CALL 911!"

AND SCENE.

STRIPTEASE

I wasn't sure what to expect when I found myself hanging out in a hotel room with half a dozen girlfriends on a weekend getaway and all of a sudden one of my friends started disrobing.

We were all chatting away, catching up, when she announced that she had something to show everyone and started lifting up her blouse. Now, given that cocktails play a dominant role in this sort of weekend, I wasn't about to rule out the possibility that my friend had not only already hit the sauce but punched it directly in the face. And no one else seemed particularly unnerved by the fact that one of us was taking off her shirt for no apparent reason, so I decided to play it cool, too.

There I was, playing it cool, as she showed her back to the

girls sitting on the bed, most of whom were smiling and saying things like "Amazing" and "Oh, wow." So I was excited
to see what she had hidden under her shirt—maybe it was a
beautiful La Perla bra, or even a tick bite that radiated indi-
cations of Lyme disease. But when she turned around, there
was no way to ever be prepared for what I saw, which was a
flaming cupcake.

Now, on any other cupcake occasion, count me in. I'll
have frosting up my nostrils in seconds flat. But in this case,
the flaming cupcake was enormous—big enough to reach
across her entire back, from shoulder blades to waist, flames
licking her spine: a gigantic tattoo, parts of which appeared
still to be bleeding.

The good news is that I did not say the first thing that
popped into my head: "Holy shit . . . that's a bloody cupcake." The bad news is that I did say the second thing
that popped into my mind, which was "You'll never make
enough money in your lifetime to get that thing removed."

After a stunned silence in which ten pairs of eyes were
on me, including those of the proud bearer of the curi-
ously behemoth cupcake, I had drawn a showstopping
blank. Looking at them, I was stunned. *Really? "Amazing"?*
I thought to myself. Our friend just ruled out any chance
of running for Congress or, however unlikely, walking a Christian Dior runway, and all you guys can say is

"Amazing"? Everyone was staring at me, and for a moment I was very confused, until I finally *got it.* Ha-ha. They were playing a joke on me. It was a joke—*a joke!* A wave of relief washed over me as I laughed at myself and replied, "Oh, thank God. It's just a decal from Hot Topic! For a minute I was scared shitless you really had a flaming cupcake etched on your back for all eternity!"

Except no one laughed back. I caught a couple of them looking silently at each other, clearly as stunned at my response as I was when I saw the Chernobyl-size cupcake. And then my friend, the one who now had a flaming cupcake etched on her back for all eternity, turned around, and with the same flames shooting out of her eyes that she had on her back, told me sharply, "It's *not* a decal."

We didn't talk much after that. She didn't speak to me for . . . well, really, ever again.

The lesson here is that a giant cupcake tattoo is typically an indication of two things: (1) Sister got her hands on some crystal meth, and (2) Sister smoked that crystal meth and kept smoking it until she had been awake for seven days and then stumbled into a tattoo parlor with a really bad idea that she had quickly sketched on a napkin from Carl's Jr.

If your friend pops up with a gargantuan flaming cupcake the size of a hubcap or medium-weight primate tattooed on her back, without question, throw her into the nearest cargo van and get that girl into rehab. *Now.* That's really your one and only option.[1] All I ever say now whenever anyone reveals a tattoo to me, whether it's an earlobe-to-collarbone declaration of "Child of the King!" scribed in Old English–type letters (exclamation point and quotation marks included) or a hummingbird that looks more like a protozoa, is, "Oh, wow. That's amazing."

---

1   This would be aside from generally advising against a back tattoo, especially since tattoo "artists" have figured out you have just paid for something the quality of which you will never be able to determine with your own eyes.

LIVE FROM THE BELLAGIO

*I*t's three o'clock in the morning, I'm in a Seattle hotel room, I've already thrown up eleven times, and the only thought left in my head after evacuating the rest of my system is: *Jesus Christ, I hate falafel.*

I didn't even want to order falafel. I didn't. I wanted to order chicken tikka masala or saag paneer at the Middle Eastern/Indian restaurant, but I only had an hour before a reading and I couldn't, in good conscience, go and talk to people with saag paneer hanging ominously on every breath I expelled. So I went with falafel; it's a safe bet, I figured—cute, contained, and, added bonus, fried! Falafel can do little to no damage, unless you count the bed of shit-tainted lettuce that it lounged upon like a concubine in a harem.

With the first bite, I had sealed my fate; by midnight, I was living the nightmare of every traveler: sweating, shivering, and leaning over a toilet in a hotel room like Kate Winslet in *Contagion,* the only movie in which she kept her shirt on, mainly because her character dies before she can get in a compromised situation with a married man.

I would have gladly taken off my shirt in front of everyone who was still alive at my thirtieth high school reunion if I could just stand up for two minutes without having to run to the bathroom like a star on *Teen Mom* hoping to score another cover of *In Touch* with rumors of another unplanned pregnancy. I was still sick by morning and, without a minute's worth of sleep, had a decision to make: call the front desk and arrange to stay another night in a hotel I could not afford, or suck it up, get myself together, and take the train home as planned.

It was then that I devised one of the worst strategies in the history of mankind. I decided that if I could keep coffee down for an hour, I was good to go for the daylong train ride back to Eugene. True, ninety percent of the coffee was French vanilla coffee creamer—which I do believe is Oil of Olay with corn syrup—but with hot tap water and a pack of instant Starbucks, I constantly strive to make things more disgusting than they ever need to be.

And in an hour, I was okay. Not so much as a gag went

down or came up in those sixty minutes—so I packed my stuff, brushed my teeth, and called for a taxi. I was so relieved I would be home in eight hours that I could hardly stand it; all I wanted to do was sweat in my own bed and drool on my own pillow.

Things were going great until I was standing in line waiting to get my ticket when I suddenly shivered and realized I had pitted out with a flash episode of perspiration that I call the IRS Sweats, the kind of horrifying chill that envelops your entire body, like when you realize you owe the IRS so much money that you have to make *payments.*

Positive I looked like a junkie with flop sweat bubbling on my face, I scanned the room to see whether anyone had noticed . . . until it occurred to me that I was in the Seattle train station. Now, I don't know if you've ever been in the Seattle train station, but I'm sure it will be a nice place someday. There will come a time when tiles won't be missing from the walls, cracked and dusty plaster won't fall from the ceiling, and yellow CAUTION tape will not stretch from crumbling wall to crumbling wall—but that day has not yet come. It does, however, make a convincing backdrop for any film featuring a drug addict/hooker/runaway character; in fact, it's the kind of place that can send anyone immediately into withdrawal. From anything.

I looked like the president of the Junior League compared to some of what was standing in line with me at the train station. In fact, I would have made a cash bet that if I suddenly yelled "Does anyone have crystal meth?" at least five people within twenty feet of me would have reached into their shoes or pants immediately. I got my bearings as the flash sweat passed and I reassured myself that once I got on the train, I would be fine. I just needed to sit down and stay down. At the ticket counter, I booked a window seat, waiting for the moment when I could rest my head against the cool glass, close my eyes, and finally sleep.

Once I walked up the tiny staircase to the upper level of the train, I found my seat, and the relief from knowing I was on my way home actually did make me feel a little bit better. I leaned my head against the window and sighed as the train started to move, slowly at first, chugging back and forth as I got closer to my own bed and my own toilet foot by foot. Jostle by jostle. By jostle. By jostle.

The first wave that rose up from my stomach only hit the bottom of my ribs and I prayed it was a gas bubble or a heart attack. I ate fried food, I told myself. It could totally be a blocked artery! I took a deep breath and tried to focus on the attendant now one row behind me, taking tickets. I got mine ready to hand over and planned to immediately make my way to the bathroom. Just to splash water on my face. That was all. Just some water.

I was *not* going to throw up.

Do *not* throw up.

Do not.

Fifteen seconds later, the next wave reached my neck but apparently did not have enough strength to surge through the several chins that I have. However, I was keenly aware of the danger that was inching forward, about to strike. I can outrun this, I told myself. I just need to give the attendant the ticket and I can run to the bathroom. I just need to hold it together for a minute. A minute is all I need. Just a minute and then everything will be fine. *A minute is all I need.*

But the conductor was busy flirting with three college girls, two sitting across the aisle from me and one next to me. I summoned all the psychic powers that I falsely claimed I had at seventh-grade slumber parties, but my fake telekinesis bounced right off the conductor and back into my face, which my hands were now covering.

Because I would rather give birth in front of people than throw up in front of an audience. At least in the former case you get to be on your pick of Lifetime shows or at minimum in a heartwarming human-interest segment about how even on a train full of strangers, everyone came together to celebrate life and paused for a second at the wonderment of it all. But vomiting in front of people? No one wants to hold that. No one cries because it's beautiful. No one can really get mad at you if your placenta splashes on their purse, but you know what? You know what happens when you throw up in front of a hundred people? Despite the fact that your hands don't know what to do except hold your mouth, as if they could effectively catch the horror threatening to spew, that third wave finds its force and rushes up like it's about to eat an Indonesian beach. And then, as if someone has just punched you in the back, before you know it, a half cup of coffee—with an excessive amount of creamer in it, I might add for the sake of detail—is suddenly riding the express car up, up, up, waiting for the signal of the most disgusting noise ever made to sound the horn of attack. It is that noise—that primitive, guttural, pathetic gag, *ehhhhh-ggggg-kkkkk*—that grabs the attention of the roughly ninety-nine people seated around you and turns their collective heads toward you to see who exactly is making that disgusting, animalistic sound.

And if there's one thing to take away from this story, if there is one lesson to be learned, it is that you should never cover your mouth with your hands in an effort to contain the spill, because that is both useless and foolish. Fanned fingers cannot catch vomit, but what they really can do is turn your little half cup of coffee (again, mostly creamer) into a spray-water feature in a fountain that rivals the Bellagio's and make it appear that your digestive system is hooked up to the city's water supply.

To be clear, I threw up on no one but myself. The coffee all landed in my lap. But that didn't stop the woman two rows ahead of me from screaming like she was on a Greyhound bus and she just saw someone get decapitated. And it didn't prevent the adorable, flirty Korean college girl sitting next to me from shooting out of her seat as if the severed head had just plopped into her lap, shrieking at full murder volume, "*I wanna change my seat! I wanna change my seat!*"

You can do a lot of things in front of people, even things unseemly, but as long as they don't see it, it's pretty much okay. The blame will always fall on the nearest baby or a person in a scooter. But it turns out you can't throw up. You can take your pants off and shoot amniotic fluid out toward them, but you can't hurl, not even on yourself. Even if the Linda Blair impression you have just performed for your fellow commuters is not your fault but rather the handiwork of an evil fake meatball, even if it's just liquid and a smaller amount than any sample size you'd get at Costco. The horrified gasps from the other passengers will fall on you like a judgment. Trust me when I say you will not know what to do in the ferocious hush that follows your public humiliation. Trust me when I say you will be frozen and stunned, like a fawn that just saw its mother get shot and then dragged onto the hood of a Chevy Silverado. Chances are good that you will simply sit there, your hands still positioned over your slack mouth. You will be stunned as if you have been through a war, and not just any war but the really, *really* bad kind, like a war of the Eastern European variety, as in Ceauşescu-level trauma.

After what feels like a generation has passed and other passengers and the conductor have still not stopped staring at you, the urge to flee will finally trigger, and 198 eyes will watch you gather up the hem of your dress like you have just been collecting vomit apples, and those eyes will follow you silently as you scurry down the aisle, other passengers recoiling on all sides as if you were handing out said vomit apples.

Dripping in puke, I staggered down the tiny train staircase and found my suitcase at the front of the car, pulled another dress out of it, and skulked into the bathroom, where I hid/vomited/sobbed/hid/vomited/sobbed for the next hour. And in some measure of good fortune—the only measure of good fortune in this story—when I finally emerged from the bathroom, which was smaller than an airline bathroom and filthier than a port-o-potty on the New Jersey Turnpike, the handicapped car was to my right. I slinked into the quiet darkness of the car, slid into an unoccupied row, and tried my very best to die.

Shortly after I took refuge in the handicapped car, where no one had seen the atrocity I had committed, the door slid open and the same conductor stepped inside to collect tickets. My cover was blown. After a brief and inappropriate thought that I should pretend to actually belong there by sitting on a leg or snatching the oxygen tank from the seat where its owner had left to go on a smoke break (and I am not kidding)—after all, I was wearing a different dress since my performance of Hurl Girl—I surrendered immediately when he came to my row. He made sure to keep his distance in case I was about to launch another splashdown, and before he could say anything, I fell on his mercy. I didn't even have my ticket anymore; it had fluttered to the ground when I scampered to the bathroom and was now resting, soaked in coffee but mostly French vanilla creamer, under the seat of an appalled, visibly shaken witness.

"I'm so sorry. Please don't make me go back up there," I begged him. "Please. I'm really sorry."

"It's okay," he said, nodding. "Lots of people get motion sickness. You can stay here and I'll bring your stuff down."

Thank you, I thought to myself, *thank you for not thinking I was a junkie and just a big dipshit spaz who forgot her*

Dramamine. I would have kissed him on the mouth if the situation had been a little different, or if I had just brushed my teeth. Or at least if I hadn't just rinsed my mouth in a train bathroom sink that was dirtier than the dress I had just changed out of.

And there I stayed for the next seven hours while that rotten little falafel ball bounced around and contaminated my system with food poisoning and chased me to the bathroom every twenty minutes. It didn't care that I was on a train. It did not care one bit. I sweated with fever, shivered with chills, and, when needed, assisted elderly and relatively immobile people to their restroom (which was cleaner than the one I had used and big enough for company), although I drew the line at helping with waistbands. I drew the line at unzipping flies in unfamiliar bathrooms, even if people with crystal meth hidden in their crotches were higher in the pecking order than I was.

I could barely sit up; my abdomen felt like I had actually used the Living Social coupon I bought for six Pilates classes but let expire because I hadn't lost enough weight to show myself in leggings yet. I had reached my lowest point of existence, I had very little else to lose.

"Begging: be at the train station @ 5," I tapped on-screen as I texted my husband in words I could not bring myself to speak into a cell phone, "bcwause cj=hances are good to excellnt that I waill have beensittign sideways for hours aftr I have shit mt pants. No longer a variable, but a cwertainty."

Before we pulled into the station in Eugene, the conductor did me one last solid and gave me this tip: "If you want to put your suitcase by the door in five minutes, you can wait there and be one of the first passengers off," he said kindly. "That way, you won't have to see anyone."

"Thank you," I said gratefully, and did just that. I was moments away from a clean escape when I looked at the person standing next to me and my mouth fell open.

"Oh my God," I said to the adorable Korean college student. "I'm so sorry. It was mostly creamer, I swear. I'm so sorry!"

Then she smiled back at me and said, "It's okay."

And I looked at her and really wanted to reply, "Well, I wish you would have said that about eight hours ago when you looked at me like I was a little dead girl with long wet hair who just climbed out of a well," but then I realized I was just about to throw up in front of her twice, so I ran into the bathroom again.

When I came out, most of the train had emptied except for the lady with the oxygen tank who already had her fingers curled around an unlit menthol cigarette. I didn't wait for her. I climbed down off the train into the heat of the afternoon and insanely bright light. I saw my husband and walked toward him, but he didn't see me until he was close enough to enter my splash zone.

"Honey?" he said to me, his eyes squinting, unsure if the green-hued creature who had just stumbled off the train with crumpled clothes, crazy Charles Manson hair, and vague traces of red lipstick smeared upward toward her right nostril was indeed his blushing bride.

"Get me to the car," I mumbled, fighting the temptation to lie down right there on the gravel along the tracks.

In a moment, we were heading for our house. We live three minutes from the train station. I was going to crawl into a motionless bed in a dark room as soon as I got there and gag without being judged by humanity. I was going to gag for the sake of gagging—gagging just to feel alive. In the meantime, on the way home from the train station, my husband looked at me sympathetically as he slowed down for a yellow light.

"My poor girl," he said, as he tapped his hand on my leg and shook his head.

"*What the hell are you doing, you idiot?*" I screamed as I sat sideways in the passenger seat, a nausea wave away from baring my teeth. "Did you not get my text? Run that god-damned light! *Run it now!*"

When I wasn't throwing up during the next two days, I was curled up in bed like a tiny zygote in my dark little room, and it took me the rest of the week to sit up without help. And even though the scars of public vomiting will take a while to heal, I know that two things will never change:

I hate falafel's stupid chickpea guts.

And every fifteen minutes when I hear a train whistle a mile from my house, I want to throw up.

WRITERS' GROUP

I have read Harry Potter erotica. Sometimes, life is like that. In one moment, you're getting ready to read what you think will be a fun little short story about a magic girl and boy and in the next, Ginny and Draco are getting it on during a study session. And three days later, while I was sitting at a small table in a cafeteria, surrounded by people I did not know, it was my turn to say something about the story to the person who wrote it.

Half an hour earlier, when I entered the cafeteria, I felt nothing but complete terror, even though I was just here on assignment from a local newspaper as an experiment. A social experiment, if you will, that raised the question of how status changes perception in art and culture. My story was only a segment of a larger feature that included what happened when a principal ballerina went for a dance audition and how the work of a renowned and respected artist was received at a street fair; I was asked to write a piece about how a published author would fare in a writers' group.

I had agreed to join this writers' workshop comprised of people I'd never met and submitted an essay for their critique. Yes, I was scared. Some writers are lovely people, but more often than not, they become insecure and *Hunger Games* competitive when hierarchy is being established in a room with more than one writer present; it's like watching wolves hash out a pecking order before tearing into a fresh kill. It is rarely pretty, and someone usually gets too drunk and is found hours later unconscious and uncomfortably close to a litter box.

I know this because I am a writer. By trade, occupation, tax forms, you name it. This is how I've made my living for a long time, decades. But none of that history has any bearing at this cafeteria table. Here, I am simply a girl named Laurie who is waiting for her essay to be led up to the workshop altar. And if the aisle up to that altar involved discussing Harry Potter porn—which I still don't get—then so be it.

"Well," I say to the woman sitting next to me, "it feels like you just had a lot of fun with this." And then I smile. I think she wants me to say more. I simply can't. Because Ginny and Draco and their naughty bits have already taken a front-row seat in my brain, blocking access to the fifty-seventh password for my iTunes account. And that is a bad thing: now I'd have to contend with images of randy wizards getting it on every time Hipstamatic comes out with a new lens to download.

"But is it *commercial*?" the older and most likely retired man across from me in the hat insists.

"Absolutely," the author replies. "*Fifty Shades of Grey* was originally *Twilight* fan fic."

Fan what? I don't know what she means and have to ask what fan fic is. The group looked at me like I was insane.

"By commercial, do you mean you intend to publish this?" I ask earnestly. "Because there might be some copyright issues with characters created by someone else." Specifically, the richest, most famous author on Earth, who I wouldn't want to tangle with in a court of law, lest everything I own, including my dog, end up in a van delivered to the Rowling house to be disposed of or used as cauldron kindling.

"I checked it out," she assured me. "It's a gray area."

"Oh," I said.

"You sure do use the word 'pussy' a lot," the man in the hat comments. Out loud.

"I'm playing off the cat in the room," the author defends.

I am dizzy. I have just read an NC-17 version of Harry

- 87 -

Potter and now an older man who I have known for fifteen minutes has uttered a word that I have been trying desperately to skip through all eleven pages of the Hogwarts porn. This is the same man who asked me when I first arrived what kind of stuff I wrote and asked for a hard copy. "First-person narrative, humor," I replied with a shrug.

He scanned the first paragraphs and then looked at me over his reading glasses. "Humor? Really?" he said as he handed my essay back to me, his face blank.

I am still feeling a little faint when we move on to the next writer, another older man with thick glasses who produces a book cover he has just paid a graphic designer to produce. It looks fantastic, although kind of young adult, with a photo of two pretty young girls and a dog in a hat.

The older man in the hat takes up the charge. "You lost me when the dog is writing a letter to the girl about how she needs to open herself up to people more," he says to the older man in the glasses. "Dogs would never do that. A dog needs to earn your trust; he never just gives it away. That's dog nature."

"No, no, no," the man in the glasses disagrees. "I don't agree. You forget that the dog is her dad, but her mother is a robot, so she has the DNA in her, too, that has no emotion. Her dad is just trying to balance that out."

"I think your cover is awesome," I say.

The man in the hat is not going to give up. "I also—I also don't understand why the dog is suddenly putting on a sports coat," he says, looking annoyed. "Where did the sports coat come from?"

"The dog wears clothes," the man in the glasses says, clearly irritated. *"That's clear from the beginning of the chapter."*

The next writer up is a woman about my age who arrived a little late, popped open her laptop, and began nodding as comments were made about her piece—which consists of the first five chapters of a novel about a film consultant/demonologist who I suspect is about to have sexual relations with a lady ghost. But I like it. There is not a single cat in the whole thing.

Others, however, find fault in several paragraphs, calling them "infodumps." (I have to ask what that is, too.) Apparently, it's when a writer gives information in a block of text, otherwise known as "backstory."

"Actually, I found your dream sequences to be very well paced and subtly done," I say. "I love the part when he blurts out that he used to be a priest. I was surprised!"

The woman looks at me and smiles. No one agrees with me.

Now it's the man in the hat's turn, and the Harry Potter lady tells him how helpful the character list was in navigating through the chapter, and when I see it, it's an entire page of characters. I'm guessing at least thirty. That's a lot for a book, let alone a chapter.

"So while I think that your opening paragraph is great with description, the next paragraph had such a vivid image with Mamoud removing his bronze, unadorned helmet," the man in the glasses says to the man in the hat. "Maybe you could switch those paragraphs and open with that picture?"

The hat goes quiet, although his eyes dart to the man in the glasses.

"No," the hat says.

I'm no psychic, but I suspect that in the coming weeks of the writers' group, there is going to be a tussle that results in one or possibly two older men on the ground with broken hips.

"Why are the two clans at war?" I ask. "I would love to know that right up front so I can understand the conflict better."

The hat laughs at me. "You have to read the whole book to find *that* out," he discloses.

"Oh." I nod.

"I loved the image of the slaves gnawing at the hides," the Harry Potter lady says. "And the space in the mouth where the rotten teeth have been pulled."

"I think at the next meeting, we should read our chapters out loud instead of reading them beforehand," the demonologist writer suggests.

"Oh, I don't think I can do that," Harry Potter says in a spray of nervous laughter. "My next chapter is rather steamy. 'Death Train' cannot be read aloud!"

"I think that's a great idea," I offer. "I find the most problems when I read my stuff out loud. And it's good practice if any of us is lucky enough to do a reading somewhere."

"I am never doing a reading," the man in the glasses informs me. "Absolutely not—I would never agree to a reading."

"Oh," I say, and nod understandingly.

And then it's my turn. I brace myself, already nervous, at the oncoming barrage.

All faces go blank when Harry Potter asks for comments on my piece.

"I didn't read that one," the demonologist says.

"I didn't, either," the man with the glasses says.

"I only read that copy you handed me," the man with the hat says.

Harry Potter crinkles her brow, shrugs, and says, "Well, I glanced through yours and had a problem telling where the rising and falling action was, but I guess I didn't upload your story to the website. Maybe we can do yours next time."

"Oh." I nod.

"All right!" Harry Potter says with finality. "So we're reading aloud next time? I'm warning you—get ready for 'Death Train'!"

And with that, everyone puts their notes away and the demonologist closes her laptop. Several people stay behind to chat, but I stick my folder in my bag, say thank you to Harry Potter, and then leave, feeling vastly insignificant and exhaling a terrific sigh of relief.

THE ACCIDENTAL PROFILER

It was ten in the morning and already the temperature was ninety-seven degrees. Waiting at a stoplight in Scottsdale at a very affluent intersection, I could see the heat rising off the asphalt like a moiré. Arizona heat, even in its infant stages before the temperature hits one hundred degrees, is unforgivable. It makes you feel like a piece of meat about to be thrown on a grill. Even I was sweating, sitting in my air-conditioned car that hadn't yet been able to recover from the hours it had been baking in the driveway since sunrise. I had nothing to complain about, however, because directly across the street on the corner was a short man holding a giant sign for a shoe and luggage repair shop in the strip mall behind him. His head was tucked under the crook of one arm; he was trying desperately to shield himself from the relentless, white heat.

I pitied him. Nobody should have to stand on the side of a busy intersection in this heat—which was only going to get worse. You see this a lot in Arizona: people doing what they can to scrape by and send a little home to the families they left behind in less lucky countries. *It's times like these that make you glad you were born in the United States,* my father's voice suddenly piped up in my head. *Greatest country in the world.*

I nodded in agreement. *He's just trying to support his family, doing whatever he can,* I thought. And the guy is so short—the sign is just a bit smaller than he is. Not only is he struggling in a strange country, but he's a miniman. Very tiny. Bet he gets in a lot of fights. I wonder why he's so short. So little. Maybe that makes it easier to get across. Do coyote smugglers charge by weight? That could be a benefit. A little silver lining on the illegal cloud. Frankly, however, I would never have children with someone that small. I wonder how small his toes are. No bigger than Good & Plentys, probably. How could you respect a man with such marginal toes? Kind of impossible. I would always be like, "Let me see your toes again. It's like they're Tic Tac toes. Are there even nails on those things?"

And then the light turned green and I drove off a mile toward my doctor's office, where I spent the next hour and a half in the waiting room, watching pregnant ladies rub their bellies while I squirmed, because everything I had just shaved was starting to grow back. After the necessary was done, I ran out of there as quickly as I could, because any time I can make it through the hall of an ob-gyn's office without someone asking when I'm due is a victory for me.

A victory that required a bagel. With cream cheese.

I was itchy.

So at around noon, I found myself stopped at the same red light in the hot intersection I had stopped at two hours before. And there, directly to my right, was the short immigrant man shielding himself from the sun with the luggage repair sign and wiping his brow on the sleeve of his black T-shirt. It was then that I noticed that the man was not a man but a boy. A little boy out in the sun at high noon, standing on a corner in one of the richest cities in our lucky country while the heat broiled him.

When the light turned green, I pulled forward slowly until I was only a few feet away from him. And sure enough, my suspicions were confirmed—there was no mistaking it. He couldn't have been older than eleven or twelve. And he looked miserable. I drove twenty more feet before I became fully enraged.

"That is a little boy!" I yelled at no one in my car. "A little boy standing on that corner holding a sign on a Tuesday at noon! Here we are, on one of the highest real estate corners in Scottsdale, and a child is out there working in the street. This isn't India! He should be in school, not standing out there in the heat for the five dollars he's going to make from that luggage repair shop!" And no one, not one person, has stopped to do or say anything about it since I drove past the first time.

"That is ridiculous!" I seconded myself. "I'm not going to stand around idle while this type of thing goes on under my nose! I am going to do something!"

"*You are?*" I whispered to myself.

"*I am!*" I answered.

And then I flipped my car into a U-turn and headed back toward the intersection by the strip mall. Just then I remembered that I had a twenty-dollar bill in my pocket. "Today is the day that a little boy doesn't have to work out in the sun," I said aloud, pointing to no one in the passenger seat, and then pulled into the next gas station.

"I am going to do something!" I nearly cried with glee. "I am going to help a little illegal immigrant boy! And I am going to tell the luggage repair people exactly what I think of them hiring a little boy to stand in the sun all day long for what probably paid pennies an hour. What kind of people were they? Who goes and picks up a little boy and makes him stand on a corner all day in the sun when he should be busy being a child, laughing at rainbows and chasing butterflies? No. There was no way I was going to let them get away with this outrage, with this atrocity. They needed to know that what they did was wrong, that this was unacceptable, and that someone had noticed *and decided to do something about it.*

When I turned into the parking lot, my plan was to verbally accost the luggage repair shop people first and then deliver twenty dollars of American freedom and a bottle of water to an overheated little boy, but then I realized I had a problem. I didn't know where this kid came from, but I had my suspicions that it was not close by. I roughly knew the area of town where the day laborers gathered in hopes of finding work—they usually met in the parking lot of the Home Depot closer to downtown, a good forty-five-minute drive from where I was. So that's like an hour and a half round-trip for me to take him all the way back there. At least six bucks in gas, seven if I put the air conditioner on high. Which I would have to do, I mean, it was only going to get hotter, and I didn't want to say to a newcomer to this country, "Well, it's just going to be hot in this car a little while longer until I drop you back off in the parking lot at Home Depot." Plus, I was meeting a friend for lunch, and I didn't want to show up all sweaty.

Or with a new, smallish friend. How would I explain that? Doctors Without Borders? I mean, I donate, but,

I'm not, like, part of it. I don't have a T-shirt or anything. Or a hat. I should have splurged for the hat. Hindsight. Damn me. *I do use the free return address labels to pay my bills, though, does that count?* Besides, there was clearly nothing wrong with him, not even a scab as far as I could see.

And the last thing I wanted to answer was the inevitable question in front of my friend: "No, I am not your new mother. I found you on the street, remember? *Y tu mamá también en* Home Depot. I know I am an American lady, but I am not Sandra Bullock. I don't even like football. I'm sorry, I don't. But it is a very good way to get to college, young man."

So that was settled. I decided to talk to the kid first, give him his rescue package, *then* yell at the luggage repair people. That seemed sensible. After all, I couldn't drag a kid—who probably didn't even know where he was going—around all day with me as he moved all the AC vents toward himself. Nope. The lecture on morals would have to wait until after I handed over the water and the money.

Confident in my decision, I got out of the car and just as quickly got right back in.

Maybe this kid is just little for his age, I realized, maybe he really just is short with teeny-tiny nailless toes, maybe he's a perfectly willing, minute-in-stature adult who would stand on a street corner while his kidneys shrivel because it's better than the circus. How would I know?

I will ask him, I decided, before I do or say anything, I will ask him, but that just provides another problem. I'd taken Spanish for a total of six years, but never got beyond Spanish 102 and retained little of what I once knew. Pulling out my trusty iPhone, I solved the problem in three seconds flat, and frankly, it didn't even come close to ringing a bell: *¿Cuántos años tienes?*

How old are you?

¿Cuántos años tienes?

¿Cuántos años tienes?

¿Cuántos años tienes? I said over and over again in my head as I opened the car door.

¿Cuántos años tienes?

Then I stopped suddenly. If he says anything aside from *ocho* and movie titles, I'm lost, I only know *ocho,* and the only reason I even know that is because we used to have a ghost in our house who used to move the tuning dial on the radio to the Spanish station every morning. We'd be woken up by the same commercial for mattresses that yelled out a phone number without mercy, *ocho ocho ocho ocho ocho ocho OCHO*!

I don't have time to memorize *¿Cuántos años tienes?* and

numbers one through eighteen, although I figured that should be self-explanatory, as in *ochoteen.*

"Problem solved!" I said, making the sound of snapping fingers in my head. I may not know his language enough for a reply, but I will indicate that he should answer by holding up his fingers. They must teach kids in every language how to do that when they're small.

I practiced in my head: *¿Cuántos años tienes?* then start flashing your fingers.

Excellent. Excellent! I would say, getting very excited.

I closed the car door and started walking across the parking lot toward the corner, the twenty-dollar bill folded up in one hand and the bottle of water in my purse. Surprisingly, I was not the only one on the sidewalk; several people stood nearby, waiting to cross the street, so I really didn't look out of place as I approached the little boy with the luggage repair sign.

I stopped in front of him and pulled my hand out of my pocket, palming the twenty. And then I summoned up all the nerve I had been telling myself for the last ten minutes that I had and stood there for several seconds before the boy's eyes met mine.

"*¿Cuántos años tienes?*" I asked slowly, flashing the five fingers on my left hand.

His eyes grew wide. He said nothing.

"*¿Cuántos años tienes?*" I said again, and flashed my fingers *louder*, but his eyes just grew wider even still. I could tell by the terror that spread over his face instantly what was going through his mind.

Aha! I thought to myself. *The luggage repair people have covered all of their bases! I get it! If a strange person says anything, they told you to be quiet! Don't answer or the police will take you away!*

"It's okay! It's okay!" I said, trying to reassure him and making hand movements that in no way indicated age *or* requested to see his ID or passport. They were simply shaky hand movements, which I was sure, had the undocumented shoe been on the other foot, I would have understood as: "I am here to help you, young man. I am not moments away from deporting you back to your oppressed and futureless homeland."

However, since we were lacking the proper avenue of communication, the look on his face shot from simple fear to utter terror, and in turn caused me to panic instead of turning to my iPhone for a helpful translation.

"It's okay," I tried to reassure him again. "I just wanted to know how old you are!"

Then I pulled the bottle of water out of my purse for some unknown reason. I suppose I felt that would prove that I was a helper with honest intentions, or maybe it was because I figured border patrol wasn't exactly known for handing out refreshments on a particularly scorching day.

Now the people waiting for the crosswalk signal were turning to look at me, most of them ready to bolt in case I started to harass them for their passports, too.

"I'm twelve!" the boy suddenly said.

And true, technically it's only two words, not very many, but it was a contraction and a number perfectly spoken in English without a trace of any foreign dialect or accent. Better spoken than if he had gone to any immersion school, I noticed. And undoubtedly, better than my iPhone Spanish. *Plus,* I thought, *I don't really know how big twelve-year-olds are, but certainly, they're bigger than this. There has definitely been some malnutrition happening here or, at the very least, the lack of a daily vitamin on someone's part.*

"Are you *sure?*" I asked him, positive I was about to foil the script the luggage repair people had laid down to cover their trek into the terrain of child slavery.

"*Yes,*" he said.

Undeterred and still heartily suspicious of a young boy standing on a street corner in the middle of the day, I surged forth, determined to finish the mission I had embarked upon.

"Why aren't you in school?" I queried, positive that this curveball was about to break the scheme wide open.

He shrugged. "I'm on spring break," he replied, his

expression of terror melting into one that consisted mainly of newfound annoyance.

"*It's Easter,*" he added, stretching his neck out in the way a prepubescent does when he considers an adult to be on the fat side of stupid.

I nodded and looked down at the water bottle in my hand. Oh, what the hell. I was already here. "You want some water?" I said, stretching out my hand to pass him the water, as my other hand with the twenty tucked into my palm went slowly back into my pocket.

"My mom just brought me some," he said, holding up not a bottle but a Tupperware jug full of water.

"So that's their store," I said, nodding over toward the strip mall. "Luggage repair."

"And shoe repair," he added, pointing to the sign in front of me.

"Wow," I said, still nodding. "That's great. I should get these reheeled, don't you think? Probably. I don't know. I shuffle a lot, I wear out the insides first. Do you know anything about that?"

He looked me straight in the eye and shrugged.

"Okay then, good-bye," I said as I hurriedly walked away, for some reason not back toward my car but forward, so that I would have to go to the other side of the parking lot, cross it, and make a complete circle before I got to my car again.

"*Hasta luego,*" he said as I walked through the gravel landscape of the bank on the corner, over several curbs, through the ATM drive-through, and over the hot, hot, hot asphalt parking lot.

As I passed the glass door of the luggage repair shop, I was never, in my life, so glad that I hadn't taken it upon myself to deliver a lecture about hiring undocumented children to work on hot street corners, as if our country were one big shoe factory instead of being so full of opportunity and promise.

But I thought I knew one thing almost for sure. As soon as the tires of my car had screeched out of that parking lot, a sweaty twelve-year-old boy most likely threw a huge sign at his mother and said, "I'm not going out there again. It's hot and a fat white lady just tried to buy me with twenty dollars and a bottle of smartwater! I want a real vacation!"

On the bright side, I'm just glad I was never in a position to have an illegal alien in my car, because I know I would have gotten pulled over for driving erratically while I tried to fairly position the air vents toward each of us, despite the fact that I was probably sweating more, and consequentially would have been arrested for human trafficking. That, and I was relieved that I didn't have to pay for another person at lunch.

I do know, however, that several months later, after ordering a burrito at a drive-through at 11:30 p.m. on a Thursday and pulling out my money to pay for it at the window, I looked at the decidedly ten-year-old boy who was working the cash register and taking orders behind the glass, put five bucks in the tip jar that was taped to the window ledge, and said absolutely nothing. Even when he said "*Gracias.*"

TINY DANCER

The first thing I need to say in my defense is that I never asked to see Anne Frank's panties. When I bought the tickets there was no mention of the possibility of seeing the tiny diarist's crotch, no indication that the sight of her undies was "without a doubt" or "unless you fall asleep." There wasn't even a disclaimer inside the playbill or an announcement before the show that the content might not be suitable for all audience members. Namely, those who might really prefer to remember Anne Frank in a certain way, like right side up.

My husband wasn't on board with the idea of spending three hours at the Anne Frank ballet to begin with, but after I told him he could go to the home-brew festival without me the following weekend, we had a deal. I wasn't really sure what to expect, because this production could have gone any number of ways. After watching pirouettes and arabesques for the first act, I was somewhat relieved that it was a regular ballet. Regular, until the usually discreet Anne Frank flashes the entire audience. I mean, the least the director could have done was put Anne in a pretty blue pair of bike shorts to make it more sporty and less . . . *Anne Frank's panties.*

Everyone knows the story of Anne Frank, and there is no changing the ending. But I'm sorry, perhaps I need a revisit, but I don't remember the Franks tumbling, rolling around on the floor, or having nightmares that, onstage, translate into something that looked like bugs getting crop dusted and involved an excessive amount of cramping and various stages of rigor mortis. Now, Margot I can see having a tumbling tantrum and Mrs. Van Daan, of course, but Mrs. Frank? And Otto? I hardly think so. *They were in an attic,* not a loft. And I think it's safe to assume that Mrs. Frank was not an acrobat by nature.

Whatever my level of disbelief with the gymnastic portion of the evening, my eyes opened further when the curtain rose on the second act and a huge gate appeared on the stage with a slew of people huddled behind it, wearing more black eye makeup than models on a Prada runway.

"*Ballet concentration camp!*" I whispered, unable to tear

my eyes away, and in a reflex move, I automatically slapped my husband's knee with the back of my hand.

"This is not worth one night of drinking beer alone," he whispered back, equally unable to turn away from the people onstage, who were now, one by one, collapsing, writhing, and apparently dying right before us. "I think I may need you to leave for the whole weekend."

For the next hour, I stifled an anxiety attack as Nazis hit people, kicked them, shot them, and were, generally speaking, acting like Nazis, but Nazis who sometimes pirouetted when the situation called for it, to their own nefarious tune. And I'm sorry, apparently I had some difficulty separating the performance part of the evening from the Nazi part. This was clear when the devils in knee-high black boots and overcoats skipped onto the stage for curtain call after the Franks died. I have to be honest and say I felt somewhat forced to clap (albeit weakly) for storm troopers who took their turns bowing.

I scanned the audience, watching everyone applaud pleasantly as the Nazis nodded and smiled. Why are we clapping for fascists? I just came to see some toe-shoe dancing, and now I'm cheering for an Axis power?

Certainly I am someone who appreciates people who work hard, especially if they're breaking a sweat, but honestly, I was having just a bit of trouble joining in on the round of good cheer for some Nazis who just killed an entire ballet troupe. The feeling did not subside after we left the theater and I saw one of the meanest Nazis, still in costume, hugging his mom, a tiny gray-haired woman in a light blue sundress, in the lobby.

I threw a look of disdain at the back of her head that said, *Frankly, you could have done a little better of a job, Nazi Mom. Did you see what your kid just did in there?*

I already knew I was in big trouble with my husband, so I thought it best to stay silent on the short drive home. I looked out the window and started nodding to a *Star Wars*–like theme song that had suddenly popped in my head. We were two blocks away from home when my husband began lightly humming a jaunty tune. I took this as a good sign; I figured if he was humming, he couldn't be that mad at me. After another three seconds of listening to him hum, I realized that it was the same little song playing in my head, and without any effort whatsoever, I jumped right in, in tempo, and hummed along with him. My husband smiled and nodded along until the grin dissolved from his face at about the same time it melted on mine.

"Holy shit," he said, our eyes locked in disgust. "That's the Gestapo song. We're singing the gestapo song!"

"*My world is upside down!*" I cried as I slapped my hand on my thigh and stomped my foot. "This is Crazy Land! I don't know who I am anymore! I just went to the ballet on half-price tickets. I didn't expect to time travel and come back a Nazi collaborator!"

"I am very disturbed by the fact that we were humming the gestapo song independently," my husband said. "Very disturbed. That's almost like a mind experiment, I feel like I have been played with! Are you sure this was a ballet and not a psychology department experimenaaaaaaaah!"

My husband sort of screamed, as much as a man who is not allowed to mow the lawn can. I followed his gaze and, in the pitch-black darkness of our driveway (because I have waited seven years for the motion detector lightbulbs to go on sale), I saw them. Four enormous, glowing, almond-shaped eyes. Enormous. Like my hand enormous. Yellow. Almond shaped. Four of them, which meant plural.

And in that moment, human instinct kicked in and I sent out my distress call, which is known as my "Conflict with Nature" sound. Apparently, I don't scream, though I am thoroughly at ease with going primitive when suddenly confronted with unknown fauna, and signaling danger as if I'm leaping from treetop to treetop on some continent where things actually leap from treetop to treetop.

"*Wooooo wooo wooooo woooooo!*" I wooooooed, I suppose to alert my own species of the unwelcome guests blocking my driveway.

I have to be honest here and admit that my initial thought was *Oh my God. Aliens!* But you have to remember, I was already traumatized by the time we pulled into the driveway. I had seen and done terrible things that evening. And if these two beasts really were aliens, then who was to stop one of them from hypnotizing us while the other one did unseemly things to us?

My husband slammed on the brakes and the headlights illuminated enough of the driveway for me to see that my extraterrestrial suspicions were incorrect. Rather than facing off with brain-sucking aliens, we had managed to box in a deer and her fawn, which were now wedged in between our neighbors' house and ours, with our car blocking their exit.

Now, a different person might have beheld the moment as a rare gift, gazing at wildlife in your front yard from the passenger seat of your car—a moment in nature that isn't often observed by people who can see a Safeway from their backyard. But I'm not that person. I'm a person from the desert of Arizona, where deer don't exist and if anything glows at night, it's a scorpion that you can throw a rock at and be done with it. I'm also the person who has seen videos on YouTube of a threatened deer taking down a fatty in a purple tank top who had been taunting him, and kicking the living shit out of a hunter who incorrectly predicted who was going to be mounted on whose den wall by nightfall.

Now, some would say my fear of these mutant woodland creatures was a silly overreaction, but I know for a fact that deer can and will run over cars and through plate-glass windows of shopping malls if the opportunity presents itself.

Sitting in the car in what I was sure were the last moments that I would have teeth, I had an immediate vision of both deer rearing up on their back legs and kicking their hooves at me like a windmill in a hurricane until my skull was smashed like a Whopper. Additionally, I am pretty sure that deer can bare their teeth and growl, because that's what I believe caused me to stop my *wooo-wooo-wooo*-ing and begin shrieking, "*Back up! Back up! Why aren't you backing up? Back up!*" until my husband put the car in reverse and floored it out of the driveway, made a sharp right turn, and sped up the hill, fleeing from our house like we had both heard the devil shout out our Social Security numbers and throw dishes at us before locking the door behind him, helping himself to snacks, making himself comfortable on the sofa, and settling in to watch *The Real Housewives*. New Jersey edition.

We were at the end of our street when my husband made a wide-angle U-turn. I looked at him as we drove three hundred feet back to our house, where he hit the curb, drove up on the sidewalk, then bounced us back into the street and slammed on the brakes with a squeal.

"What are you doing?" I said after my brain settled back into place.

"Maybe they left by now," he assessed, scanning the bushes for those amber alien eyes peeking through the shrubbery.

"We've been gone for six seconds," I informed him.

"Just run to the front door," my husband said, gently pushing me toward the door with his hand on my shoulder.

"Oh my God!" I shrieked, pulling away. "Are you serious?"

I quickly had a vision of myself making it two steps out of the car before a frothy-mouthed Bambi leaped from the rhododendrons and used my face as a punching bag, while I curled into a fetal position and attempted to roll toward my porch like a pill bug, as my husband shouted encouraging but muffled words from the driver's seat through closed car windows.

"I'm not Sigourney Weaver," I said slowly with a sly grimace. "And I am not the last one left on this ship in deep space. I will stay here until help comes."

"Help?" my husband questioned. "What, are you going to call animal control? Is there a deer catcher? 'Hello, Deer Catcher? There are two woodland creatures in my driveway that I initially mistook for extraterrestrials. Yes, I saw *Fire in the Sky,* too. So you can understand my apprehension. They did unholy things to that man. That was a true story! We've actually been to that area, you know. It was in Arizona. We're from Arizona. I know. *I know.* I think that governor is a nut, too! You should hear her on the radio, she has some pretty crazy mouth sounds. You would think that a governor could afford better-fitting dentures. They sound like they're going to slide out of her mouth like a bar of soap!'"

I gasped and my mouth stayed open, accusatorily. "*I would totally stay on message in a time of crisis,*" I hissed. "And I resent your implications otherwise."

My husband cleared his throat. "Come on. You go first."

I shot him an incredulous look, mouth agape. "You have got to be kidding me."

He pressed on: "I saw three-quarters of Anne Frank's buttocks tonight while her father lifted her up inappropriately while she did the upside-down splits above his head," he said clearly. "Someone needs to pay for that."

I looked away and took a moment, eyeing the front door as I calculated the distance up the walk.

Then I opened the passenger-side door and, recalling a recent Liam Neeson movie I had seen on cable, ran to the front door with my house key poised in between my index and middle fingers in case I needed to suddenly stab a deer in the neck.

Though armed with what essentially amounted to a long fingernail, I was still caught off guard when the moonlight reflected off one gigantic retina staring me down through the rhododendron bush as I neared the front door. Moments away from having my skull crushed like an eggshell, I felt adrenaline shoot through my body so fast that it made me dizzy; the keys tumbled out of my hand and landed with a tinny clatter on the concrete steps of the front porch.

"Keys! Grab the keys!" my mind screamed at me, as my hands sliced through the air like a feather through tar. "Get the keys! That thing is going to kick you in the back of the head, and if there's one thing you don't need, it's another head injury. One more blow to the head and that's it. You'll be in diapers and on a leash in a dayroom somewhere, probably in Arizona. I can't feel my legs. Jesus, I have to go to the bathroom!"

I grabbed the keys, flipped through them like a madman, repeatedly glancing back to keep an eye on my pursuer, and finally found the one for the front door just as the big eye blinked, ready to attack, and I froze. The deer took a step forward and I winced, trying to fold my body inward, bracing it for blunt-force trauma. As I waited for my fate, the creature took a step behind me, then another, and another, sauntered across my lawn, in front of my husband, who was encapsulated within the safety of our car, and then swaggered slowly up the hill like a model on her last runway. Her fawn followed with a spring in her trot, bounding around as only babies, unaware of the danger around them at all times, can. This time that danger was represented by a lady in a body shaper that had rolled so far up both legs, it looked like a Speedo and cut off circulation to the point of tingling.

The next week, when I opened the envelope that contained my tickets to the opera *Nixon in China,* I smiled slightly, thinking, *How bad could it be? I mean, I did get them for half price.*

Plus, I hear Chairman Mao has a solo.

FABRIC OBSESSION

*T*he moment I walked through the front door when I came home from my sewing class, I saw it. There was no mistaking it, and I immediately felt the flush of anxiety rush up from my stomach and swallow my head in a fiery gulp.

On the side of the box, in bright blue and hideously large letters, its origin was declared.

"You got another box from Fabric.com," my husband said from the couch without looking up from his book.

I nodded and fake smiled, trying very hard not to betray my panic and to remain as calm as possible.

Normally, I love getting mail—packages in particular. I love it so much that I rarely stop to think about what I look like before I answer the door, a character flaw that I am powerless to change. A package is a package. The UPS man assigned to my route clearly drew the short straw, as I've been known to throw open the door in my bathrobe looking like a Lady Alcoholic on her way to Rite-Aid to kill her six-pack bag full of three-dollar chardonnay because I was so excited to claim my prize. The problem with this particular box was that I didn't remember buying anything recently.

I cast a furtive glance over my husband's head at the four-foot pile of totes and boxes, all containing fabric, in my Hoarder's Corner and ferreted the box into the kitchen. I set it down on the kitchen table and eyed it suspiciously. This new box horrified me. How could I be so far gone with my fabric obsession that a purchase just got lost in the mix to the point that I didn't even remember the delight of buying it?

A hobby is only as good as its accessories, and sewing barely has any competition in that area. After all, the reason I have so much fabric is because I love it. I'm not proud of it, but I will admit to making monkey sounds and flapping my arms like a heron when I encountered a particular brown-and-red pin-striped wool for thirty-five dollars a yard. (A yard, by the way, is not enough to make anything for a person with an ass my size.) I cooed over it like it was a baby I gave up in order to go to college instead of going on food stamps. It was ridiculous and deteriorated from there when I bought as much of it as I could afford (a yard).

So when you take someone who loves something so much that her inappropriate emotional response to it nearly caused her to hover and *then* tell her she can make a dress out of it, the game is over. By the time I brought the pin-striped fabric home, both sides of the armoire and former DVD cabinet were filled with wool, faille, crepe, challis, and silks. I had one box of patterns. Then two. Then three. I departed one day for Costco on a cheese and wine mission and came home with totes for "storage." Boastful, foolish girls in my sewing class bragged about how they were making a dress out of a sheet they got at Goodwill for three bucks, but I had Vera Wang faille I scored on Fabric.com for $3.99 a yard, plus a thirty-percent-off coupon code. Eight yards of it in case I wanted to make two dresses from it, neither of which would make me look like a sister wife who had spent three bucks on a dirty sheet from Goodwill when I put them on.

And then Fabric.com had the entire Ralph Lauren fabric selection on sale and the totes filled up at the end of my bed. Herringbone. Taffeta. Plaid suiting. And on one lucky score, cashmere. One day, the UPS driver handed me several Minuteman missile–size objects as he averted his eyes in case I was dressed like a middle-aged version of Sandy in the last scene of *Grease* again. Bolts of Vera Wang satin. Buck ninety-nine a yard. *That's like putting cocaine on sale.*

Of course I was going to buy two bolts of twenty yards each! I'd be insane not to.

If that wasn't bad enough, when I went back to Phoenix to visit my family, I rediscovered SAS, a fabric remnant store and the glories contained within each location, despite the brusque, gruff Eastern Bloc women who worked there; I suspect they have been kinder in cutting the throats of goats than in answering your questions. While digging through the piles of fabric for $2.99 a pound (that's right, a pound; cocaine for $2.99 a pound—Pablo Escobar never got it so cheap, and cocaine doesn't drape as nicely as a good dupioni does), I actually found a piece of fabric I had returned to Fabric.com two months before, the sticker still on it. It was the same stuff I had been buying online, but now it was even cheaper!

On one particularly fruitful trip to SAS, I bought so much cotton velvet, plaid wool, and high-end rayon ($1.99 a pound! That's cheaper than expired Albertsons ham!) that I had to drag the bag to the car and wrestle it into the front seat like it was a thirty-two-dollar corpse with great nap. I put the contents in the first tote that broke ground in Hoarder's Corner and began to spend so much time at SAS that on one memorable occasion, the woman who looked like she had lived through the most wars let me use her hand sanitizer and almost cracked a smile when I made a joke about the trim section being a bigger mess than the country formerly known as Czechoslovakia in 1992.

Hoarder's Corner grew to multiple levels, the penthouse being an enormous box from Fabric.com with those telltale blue letters on the side, big enough that I debated adding a pillow to it and using it as a napping box. But even when the corner began to crown above the couch with boxes and bags of fabric, reaching proportions that prompted my husband to ask whether I was planning on moving somewhere, I wasn't that alarmed. It was just messy, I told myself, a problem that could be easily remedied when I cleaned out a "little shelf in my closet" to relocate the five-foot-by-five-foot fabric monument.

But when I saw the mysterious Fabric.com box as I walked through the door after sewing class, everything changed. I suddenly had the feeling that I needed to call Candy Finnigan and book a suite at the Red Lion Inn, because my episode was next up on *Intervention*. This was serious. How much fabric did I really need, anyway? I don't buy anything I don't love, but apparently, I have a lot of love to give and it's clearly exclusive to textiles. I had more than I needed. I had more than I would ever use. I had more than sweatshops in India. And I suddenly mourned for the children with tiny fingers that I never had.

It took me approximately two hours to even get close to opening the box, but eventually, curiosity and my fabric-whore proclivity got the better of me. I sliced open the box and pushed the cardboard flaps aside. The contents were encased in a plastic bag, and I eagerly rifled through it to see what I'd bought and had no memory of buying. Was it silk? Was it the piqué I had waffled over for several weeks? Was it the polka-dot voile I was waiting to go on sale?

And then, there it was. A pair of eyes. A hairy chin. A large forehead, not unlike a former boyfriend's. It was an embroidered portrait of Bigfoot and was accompanied by a vintage pattern for a Western shirt, and bags and bags and bags of vintage-class buttons. The card inside wished me a happy birthday and was signed by my friend Lore in California, who is almost a bigger fabric whore than I am, and whose tower of fabric boxes had occupied a corner, then a closet, until she went big-time by convincing her husband that she needed an even bigger house with her own sewing room. Despite the glory of her victory, she had still taken the opportunity to hide her own slutty fabric ways by sending the evidence to my house via my birthday present.

But it's okay. I took a deep breath, exhaled a big puff of relief, wandered over to my pile of Fabric.com boxes, and looked at the box that was the foundation for my tower. Even though a part of me had truly fantasized about curling up inside of the enormous box big enough to throw a pillow inside and take a nap in, it would be perfect for sending the pair of earrings I got Lore for her birthday the following week.

THE GUANTÁNAMO BAY
KNITTING AND BOOK CLUB

*I*t's 4:45 a.m., and a woman in polyester pants has just stuck her hand in my crotch.

Several people stop and stare unabashedly, their mouths hanging the slightest bit open. I can't blame them, I probably would have stared, too. Of course, it doesn't help matters that I am screaming.

An hour earlier, my husband pulled up to the curb and kissed me good-bye; I was on my way to a writing conference in Idaho and wasn't all that happy about getting up so early to catch my flight. But I live in a small town with a smaller airport, and it usually takes three flights and an equal number of Ativans to deliver me wherever I need to go, so I have to get started early in the morning. I typically don't mind traveling, as long as I don't remember it.

As I dragged my suitcase into the airport, I instantly sighed in complete dismay. The security line was long, longer than I had ever seen it, but I knew I had enough time to make the flight. It's just that being awake at 4:45 in the morning is enough of an offense without being made to shuffle forward two steps at a time like a mental patient in socks.

I got in line, got my boarding pass and ID in order, and waited. And waited, and waited. The line was barely moving, and as I peered around the others in line ahead of me, I saw why. Only one lane was open as opposed to the usual two at the Eugene Airport—and that wasn't all. The Eugene Airport had gotten a new toy courtesy of TSA, in the form of a monolithic Rapiscan imaging machine, and it was not a nice one that only blows at you. It was the one that sees you naked.

I was shocked. Why a little town like Eugene, Oregon, needed a naked scanner was beyond me. I've seen most of my fellow Eugenians naked at one point or another, and not by choice. They'll throw on a loincloth and join a drum circle without hesitation, and there're always at least a dozen women on hand in any locale who would jump at the chance to unbutton their shirts and breastfeed a hungry baby or kindergartener who was in need of refreshments. Frankly, what this town needs more than a Rapiscan image machine is a Bra Fairy. We need to tie up some of those low-lying boobs like boats before a hurricane, not put them on a screen. The last thing Eugene needs is more nudity, especially at the airport.

Because at small-town airports, the TSA people take their jobs very, very, very seriously, just as, say, a lone deputy might in a town with one jail cell. Hey, terrorists can come from anywhere, right? Never mind that ninety-eight percent of my fellow residents in Eugene can't operate a debit card terminal and will wait five minutes while the cashier asks her manager if the lettuce at Five Guys was organic (save yourself five minutes: the answer is NO). Sure, these are people whose biggest crimes are painting streetlamps rainbow colors in the middle of the night and yarn bombing bike racks, so I could see how it would be merely a hop, skip, and a jump for these people to strap explosives to their privates, particularly if they were locally grown.

This is the same airport, mind you, that flagged me for a luggage search when I was about to leave for a three-week-long book tour. When you're going away for that long, you have to be careful about packing, and each piece fits like a puzzle. It's a house of cards, and if you pull one piece out, the whole enterprise collapses. Carefully, and with the utmost spatial economy in mind, I placed twenty-one fiber-drink packets side by side in a pocket and was able to lay them flat, and was carefully closing my suitcase as my husband walked by.

"Oh, good luck with that!" he said, pointing to the twenty-one little tubes lined up like soldiers. "That doesn't look like dynamite or anything."

"You're an idiot," I said as I gingerly laid the suitcase cover down and zipped it up.

Two hours later, standing in front of a stainless-steel table at the airport, I was watching a strange man with white hair and fat fingers destroy my maxipad-and-underwear pyramid when I decided I'd had enough.

"If you're looking for the dynamite," I advised, "it's in the side pocket."

He looked at me sharply, keeping an eye on me as his knotted hands groped the side pocket and he withdrew a packet.

"What is this?" he asked me sternly.

"It's a fiber drink," I informed him.

"Why do you have so many?" he questioned briskly.

"I'm on a book tour for three weeks," I explained. "And it's easier than packing twenty-one bean burritos."

"They resemble explosives," he added, still not taking his hard stare off me.

"Consumed in careless amounts, you are absolutely right," I agreed.

He tried to shove the fiber packet back into the pocket

like someone who's never been on a book tour for three weeks. My careful fiber row collapsed, spilling into the well of the suitcase in a huge heap. I was going to have to completely repack, which was evident the moment I saw him dig into my suitcase like a badger.

"Is that all the fiber?" he asked. "Is there any more?"

You know, this is getting a little gastrointestinally personal, I wanted to say. *When's the last time* you *ate a vegetable*? But I had already mentioned the word "dynamite," and even though Guantánamo Bay actually sounds like more fun than a book tour, I decided to cooperate.

"Yes," I confessed. "There are gummy fiber bears tucked between my girdles and there are some stool-softener gel caps in the first-aid pocket. Thank you. You now know me more intimately than my husband."

He tried to close the top of the suitcase and then slid the whole mess over toward me. "You're a writer?" he asked.

"Yes," I answered, trying to line all of my fiber soldiers back up again.

"What book did you write?" he continued.

"The book you just bent the cover to when you were digging your way through the Kotex section of my suitcase," I informed him.

"I write science fiction," he said, and suddenly gave me a little smile. "Can you help me get a book published?"

I smiled back, zipped the suitcase up as best I could, and then yanked it off the table.

"Nope," I said as I walked away.

It was clear that things hadn't changed—the Eugene TSA was still taking things very, very seriously, even more so with the new naked machine. I had been in line for at least twenty minutes and had barely moved, and once I paid attention to what was going on in front of me, I understood why.

There were children lined up at the naked machine; many, many children. Most of them looked to be middle-school aged, about fifteen to twenty of them, accompanied by three chaperones. All of them were deaf, or had hearing aids that were setting off the machine, and the TSA was in something of a tizzy. They were shouting to the kids to step into the machine and put their hands up for the imaging to take place, but it was all going horribly wrong. As a result, some of the kids were getting frisked and others stood confused in front of the machine as the TSA haplessly shouted directions. It was a mess. And time was ticking.

The security line was now incredibly long, and by the time I got even close to the machine, I had only twenty minutes until takeoff. I tossed my suitcase on the conveyor belt, and this time (I had learned my lesson), as the fiber packets were resting in my purse. I took off my shoes and waited next in line to be blasted by naked rays.

The guy in front of me passed through without a hitch, and I was glad; I barely had enough time to run to the gate and catch my flight. When the TSA agent called "Next!" I stepped into the machine and put my feet in the designated space and held my hands up when I was instructed to. I did not even breathe, not wanting to cause the least bit of delay.

When I exited the machine, I began to walk over to fetch my suitcase, but the agent stopped me.

"Female!" he yelled, and in a minute, a woman in a ponytail and wearing polyester pants came up to me and asked me to spread my arms.

Shit, I thought.

"Do you have any metal in your body?" she asked me, to which I answered no.

"Are you sure, ma'am?" she said sternly, clearly not believing me. "There seems to be some metal in your torso."

"Um, no," I said, shaking my head. "My underwire bra, maybe?"

"This appears to be in the rib area," she informed me as she started patting me around my midsection.

"I don't have a metal rib," I assured her.

"And in the left hip? What do you have there?"

"Pardon me?" I asked as she continued to pat. "Nothing. I have a real hip. I have no metal in my body."

"That's not what the scan says," the agent replied, patting down my boobs with the backs of her hands.

"I don't have metal in my body," I reiterated. "I have real ribs and an arthritic hip."

"Stand with your feet apart, please," the woman said.

I just wanted this to move along. I positioned my feet on the yellow footprints on the rubber mat.

And then it happened. Her hand was patting my ass, and then, suddenly, it was in my crotch.

I turned my head suddenly, trying to determine if that had really happened. IN my crotch, like I need to be married to you *in my crotch*. Or like you'd better have a degree from a medical school in the United States *in my crotch*. Like I'm having a baby in the back of a cab, I didn't even know I was pregnant and you're the only one who can help me, mister, *in my crotch*. But not like you're a lady with two semesters of community college, you have a scrunchie in your hair and you think I am lying about having a metal rib *in my crotch*. Because that kind of *in my crotch* is not cool. It is not cool with me. I've been frisked before, the full pat down, several times, in fact, and this was different. This was . . . extensive. Now, sure, I was naturally wearing the tightest spandex sausage casing known to the female gender,

THE POTTY MOUTH AT THE TABLE

and I was as taut as a full helium balloon or a vacuum-sealed ball of mozzarella. But believe me, if I had a cookie bomb shoved into my girdle, you could not spell yeast infection fast enough, and that's enough of a deterrent for me to reject being a terrorist.

"Um," I started to say.

"Ma'am," the agent said again as she came around to my side. "Is there metal in your hip?"

"No, there is not," I said, as firm as I dared. "I don't know what scan you are reading, but it's not mine."

"It's yours," she said, running her hand down the outside of my leg, and then back up the inside of my leg and right back to ground zero. Where she had clearly just been.

"Okay," I said, without a thought, and then added, "That's enough. That is enough."

She went back down the other leg and then back up again.

"This is unnecessary," I said, louder, and without any control over my mouth, because once, twice, three visits to the same region was enough to flip the switch, and the only reason the switch didn't get flipped on the first visit was because, yes, I was on Ativan and my delay times were appropriately slow. Normally, if you stick your gloved hand into my high-rent parts without proper authorization once, you'd get a tooth knocked out. Three times and I'd be sucking the eyeballs out of your face and spitting them back at you.

From behind me, she went back a fourth time, and that was when I, knowing better, knowing that I could be detained and cuffed and held by the authorities for standing up for myself, began to yell, "I demand that you stop. This is unnecessary! You are violating my civil rights! *You are violating my civil rights!*"

But I couldn't stop myself. It was impossible. And that's when people stopped and stared. But I said it again, and again, and again, until she finally dropped her hand and walked away.

"That was bullshit," I said loud enough for the people now watching me to hear. "She did not need to touch me like that. It was bullshit."

And then I waited. I waited to be led away to some windowless al-Qaeda room where I would not be read my rights because in an airport security line, you simply don't have any. *Oh well*, I thought, *it might not be so bad*. I could start a knitting club at Gitmo; I mean, everyone needs a prayer rug and a beanie, right? That could be fun. Or maybe a book club, or, more accurately, the Quran Club, that might be enlightening—it's probably better than *The Help*. Just trying to look on the bright side here, because man, I really friggin' hate hummus. And falafel. Oh, falafel.

But no one came. No one took my arm. No one said, "This way, please, Metal Rib Bomber." I was just there by myself, with my arms outstretched, standing on a mat with my feet spread. The people in the security line went back to gathering their shoes, suitcases, laptops. I found my boots at the end of the conveyor belt, along with my purse that had five packets of fiber powder in it, and my artfully packed suitcase. I gathered everything up, and pulled on my boots.

I got to my gate just as my plane was shooting down the runway, then tilted upward and lifted off into the sky.

BUSTED

Dear Municipal County Clerk:

Let me start by saying I am sure you don't have an easy job. I suppose that's apparent by the fact that you have to sit behind shatterproof glass, which says to me that you have your share of irate customers on a daily basis, and you probably see crazier things and touch dirtier objects than the girl who works the return counter at Walmart.

However, just because you deal with people paying their fines and court fees as a result of lawlessness does not entitle you to jump to conclusions about every formerly law-abiding citizen who steps up to your window. Law-breaking is a spectrum, you know, with all sorts of colors in between. *Not every color is jumpsuit orange.* So when you look at my citation with a clearly disparaging look and

say, "Whoa!" I take issue with that response for a variety
of reasons:

1. Reserve your disdain, sir, for those who actually take the
law into their own hands and who were not really speed-
ing but, more accurately, going downhill and submitting to
the forces of physics. I didn't invent physics; I didn't vote
for physics; I don't even *understand* physics. I was simply
going downhill on a road made by *your employer,* the city,
and I can hardly be held responsible for the grade it deemed
appropriate. Apparently they signed off on a perfect physics-
fed speed trap that I believe was solely created as a money-
making venture for the city, like a police-staffed lemonade
stand.

2. Doing 43 miles per hour in a 35-miles-per-hour zone is
not breaking the sound barrier, m' lord. It's not like I was
all gassed up and making my way to Mars in a Prius that in
certain moments gets 99 MPG. *Ninety-nine miles per gallon*
sometimes, even if it's just for a fraction of a second. If that
doesn't demonstrate how seriously I take my responsibility
to humanity, including people overseas who I do not understand when they call me to tell me my credit card payment is
late, then frankly, I don't know what does. I had a V6 Camry
before I decided to provide a future for children I don't even

have, so it's clear that I traded speed and power for a car that everyone who volunteers for Habitat for Humanity drives, and even some Doctors Who Don't Have Borders.

a. I was not drunk. Nor was I cited for that, but I could see the look of speculation that crossed your face when you saw my speed of eight miles above the posted limit. "What sort of madwoman *is this*?" it said. *Stand down, sir.* Stand down.

I will have you know that for most of the summer, we have had our teenage nephew staying with us, and whenever I got a little too happy at breakfast, lunch, or dinner, all I had to do was toss him the keys and my chances of walking the line dropped dramatically. Sure, sure, it was my plan to wait a week before I drank "magic grape juice" in front of the Mormon side of the family, but happy hour is happy hour and if there's a three-dollar glass of chilled rosé calling my name on a summer afternoon, you can hardly expect me to ignore that sort of value. Alcohol rarely goes on sale. But I can usually find it when it does.

b. Yes, it's true that I did not have my proof of insurance with me at the time of the bust, but that was only because State Farm sends me a letter every other day describing what horrors and lawsuits could befall my household, and I simply cannot live in a world of fear like that. That is too much stimuli, and I can't keep worrying about wiping spilled orange juice off my floor every time I leave my house in case a crackhead breaks in, slips in the kitchen, and hurts himself. Or if a hobo sidles into my backyard, goes to take a poop in my vegetable bed, a rusty trellis scrapes his ass, and he needs a tetanus shot.

Straight into the shredder the anxious State Farm envelopes go, so I can't keep track of when the new cards come! I had more expired State Farm cards in my wallet than I did receipts from Cinnabon, and that became clear when I scraped a little bit of paint off my car while I was trying to parallel park last week.

Normally, I am an excellent parallel parker, but there was a man standing next to my car who was watching me intently (yes, I would use the word "staring"—he was staring) and it threw my concentration entirely off until he yelled at me, "Hey! You just hit my car!" which really derailed any sort of focus I had left.

c. *Look at me.* Really. *Look at me.* I was the only one in the entire court, including some of your coworkers, who did not have a neck or facial tattoo, or who was not wearing a tank top and flip-flops. I was wearing a full slip and a body shaper, for your information, proof that I was the only one in that entire building who was adhering to the full rules of society!

I even had lip liner on; how many times have you seen that in a mug shot, unless it's of a tranny or someone who just stabbed her pimp? *Hardly ever.* And you know what? Don't keep turning over my credit card like it was a cantaloupe to see if it's bad. It's perfectly fine. It is. It's not like you're going to find a soft spot if you palm it enough. It is fine. The lady from India called just yesterday and we got my payment all taken care of. Run that thing, buddy. You just run it.

So those are the things that I felt needed some clarifying. I hope you see a broader picture now and aren't so quick to judge a person just because she was driving eight miles an hour faster than the Volkswagen bus next to her covered in a cloud of toxic fumes and missing a muffler. Yeah. *That guy* didn't get a ticket. That guy isn't having his credit card fondled, because that guy would never show up in court. He's too busy breaking all the other boundaries of society, like not wearing a shirt while driving on a public road and turning the sky black with cancerous exhaust, to even know there was a speed limit and that he was traveling twenty miles an hour miles under it.

Awesomely,
Laurie Notaro

PS: Working behind glass doesn't make you more brave, you know. It doesn't. It just makes me want to ask you for one adult ticket to the matinee.

THANKSGIVING!!!!

*L*ast year when my neighbor Louise asked us whether we'd like to join her family for Thanksgiving, I almost kissed her on the lips. But I had to get some vital information before I puckered up.

"Is butter allowed?" I asked.

"Yes . . . ?" she replied, looking a little puzzled.

"Are the rolls made out of rice flour?" I queried.

"Eww! God, no!" she answered.

"Any other carnivores coming?"

"Of course!" She laughed. "Me!"

It was a huge relief, mainly because I was still a little shell-shocked from the previous Thanksgiving. Actually, that was putting it mildly. I was so wounded that I couldn't pass sliced turkey at the deli counter at Safeway without wanting to use a carving knife for very bad things.

The previous year wasn't the first Thanksgiving I had hosted; I was a veteran at getting a huge dinner together for the orphaned and lonely graduate students and colleagues of my husband's who made up our circle of friends in Oregon. But as we all counted down the years we had lived in Eugene, strange things began to happen. Things began to change.

At one happy hour, a friend ordered a Gardenburger. During a bowling excursion, someone refused the community cheese fries and then made a frowny face, shook her head, and rubbed her belly. Another friend looked at the pizza that had just arrived at our table during a birthday celebration and said simply to the waitress, "I can't eat that! Can I just get a side of olives?"

This is what happens when you drink too much at social gatherings; you don't put the pieces of the puzzle together until you start inviting people to break turkey with you and you find out who it is they've become. At first, a couple of them converted to vegetarianism, which is fine: there's no meat in pumpkin pie and I just made more green beans. Then came the confession of intolerance, and in Eugene, that means no dairy, no gluten (also known as no joy in life, and it shows). Then the ultimate, which almost felt like a complete betrayal: "We are Vegan, and that's with a capital *V,* thank you very much, pet eater."

I spent almost two days making three versions of each dish to accommodate all of our guests. Mashed potatoes with olive oil and garlic. Sweet potatoes with maple syrup and almond butter. Pumpkin pie with agave and rice flour pastry. I had to buy something with the word "namaste" on it. Did you know that gluten-free rolls are eight bucks a bag? Did you? And do you know what vegans bring to Thanksgiving? Hummus. Hummus and nut crackers, and believe me, when you look at your dining room table and there are twelve tubs of beige shit, it is very clear that there is such a thing as too much frigging hummus.

In the end, the bathroom was the most popular spot that holiday as the dishes got mixed up (or purposefully ignored) and the dairy-free people ate the real mashed potatoes, a green bean accidentally grazed a piece of dead fowl, and the rolls and the hummus went absolutely untouched. Then someone announced she was allergic to wine and did we have any Martinelli's?

Allergic to wine?

I made a vow then that if we were ever going to host another Thanksgiving, it was simply going to be a platter of Lactaid and Imodium A-D.

So when Louise asked us to her house for the holiday,

I breathed a sigh of relief. She had just saved me a big trip to the pharmacy and the urge to bludgeon a sulfite-adverse hippie with a wine bottle.

"We'd be delighted to come to Thanksgiving," I told Louise. "Any chance for a hummus shoot? I still have eight containers in my fridge."

NETTLE MIND

All right. It's high time someone stood up and said something. And no one else seems to be making a move, so here I go.

For the second time in a week, I've seen nettles on a menu.

Nettles.

This is what I know about nettles: they invaded my front yard last year to the point that I'm sure I poisoned my portion of the water table trying to eradicate them; they have stinging hairs that make them the Chinese stars of plants; and I don't want to pay twenty-two dollars a plate for them.

Now, I know it's on trend for chefs to incorporate nontraditional ingredients into their cuisine to add unexpected elements and ingenuity to their dishes. I know it's important to shake things up in the culinary world to drum up some excitement and entice people to dine out instead of cooking the same old meals at home. I mean, how many ways can you fry a chicken? (As it turns out there are only two: good and not good.) Unfortunately, some of the more inventive restaurants attract the sort of people who say reprehensible things like "Those two flavors play on my tongue, basking in their season" or "The wine tasted like jam and sunshine," thus making asses out of themselves on Urbanspoon.

Don't get me wrong, I'm not so old-fashioned that I want all of my meals served in aspic. But every now and then, the trends start going a little haywire (the Wedge, anyone? It's a quarter of a head of iceberg lettuce and a teaspoon of Hidden Valley for $6.99 at a chain restaurant near you). I will be the first one to admit that I'm not a foodie and no ingredient has ever "basked in its season" or "played on my tongue"; I just like to eat and I know good food when I chew on it. Bad food makes me angry; silly food sends me into a rage. Yelp makes me want to put out hits on people. And I'm starting to see an awful lot of silly food creeping onto the menus of some of my formerly favorite restaurants.

It's happened gradually, as all poxes do, the weirdness creeping into the food like weeds until there is nothing left on the menu that I want to order at a restaurant I used to love. For example, creamed rabbit makes my throat spasm and my hand fly to cover my mouth while I dash for privacy, and if I wanted to eat a pigeon, I would have learned how to use a slingshot when I lived in Phoenix; it would have solved a droppings problem, too. Seriously. I'm not eating pigeon. Or veal cheeks, or pig's stomach, or parts of a little lamb's brain. While I agree that all are great conversation starters, I'd rather stand by the punch bowl and talk about the felonies I've committed than admit that I just ate things the Donner party wouldn't have considered.

I suspect this trend of exploratory cuisine is rolling to a fever pitch because everybody who ever boiled water wearing a paper hat wants to be on *Iron Chef* or *Top Chef Masters,* and one way to stand out is to serve what no one else is serving—whether it's lion from a supplier who was once convicted of selling federally protected animals or the mouth of a pig, with or without lipstick. Throw stuff that should be ground into sausage straight onto the grill and make a sauce for it. Froth up a nice, spitlike foam and people will think you're a genius.

But it's not genius or inventive or even showboaty. It's just silly.

The thing is this: My grandfather got on a boat in 1914 and sailed from Italy to New York City in hopes of making a better life for his family for generations to come. I'm nearly positive that when he reached Ellis Island, the reason he gave for coming to America was so that his son, his grandchildren, and all of his descendants would never have to eat pigeon. *Never.* If he'd been served nettles back then, he would have turned right around and got back on the boat. I can picture him storming out, crying: "Nettles are bullshit! I didn't come all the way here to eat a garden pest that leaves splinters in my mouth! This is America. Give me a tenderloin!"

Nettles are things you eat when the potatoes get blight before you can pull them out of the ground. Pigeon is something you attack when every other animal has already been eaten. These are foods of last resorts. It's the menu for the apocalypse. And while I can appreciate the objective of butchering an animal and using all of it, isn't that the precise reason we shove things in casings, tuck them into buns, and squeeze ketchup all over them? Everything gets used, really, *I promise.* I've eaten pig lips before and so have you, I'm certain of it. We just didn't know it because it plumped when we cooked it.

Frankly, I'm sorry to say that there's nothing smart, nouveau, or exciting about eating the things our ancestors ate when they were hungry, poor, and couldn't afford the decent cuts of meat. It's the same food they sailed across an ocean to escape.

Just consider this a warning before your favorite restaurant goes a little beastly and tries to slip hooves onto their menu. Even if it has marmalade pesto foam on it, refrain. The day may come when you have to eat a foot.

Today, however, is not that day.

I HATE FOODIES

$\mathcal{S}$ome people, such as readers of Eatocracy, followers of food blogs, and Food Network devotees, consider themselves inductees into a special club of "culinary provocateurs," whose standards have risen so far above your average chewers that they have closed ranks and invented their own language, like twins who didn't eat each other in the womb or a feral Jodie Foster living secretly in the woods.

Chicka, chicka, chickabee.

Anyway, here are the most horrific examples of foodie speak. We all have to eat; but when you start acting kinda Big Ike about it, you ruin it for everybody. Naturally, I believe a punishment schedule should be enforced so the rest of us don't have to tolerate this nonsense as it invades menus, cooking shows, and conversations overheard from the asshole in the booth behind us who will soon be the victim of a spoon-related attack if he doesn't shut his piehole, mark my words. If you can understand them.

I'd like to permanently strike the following vocabulary from the record, posthaste. (That's big-shot for "starting now." See how that word just sucked the fun out of that whole sentence? That's what foodie speak does.)

Amuse-bouche

Thanks, Padma Lakshmi, for bringing this gem to the forefront when you could have just said "appetizer" or, even more truthfully, "jalapeño popper." Now every guy who owns a can of hair fixative is busy telling his guests that spray cheese on a Triscuit is something superclassy, like dip in a bread bowl. Amuse your own mouth, Padma, you have an illegitimate baby. You do.

Punishment: Being forced to eat dip *and* the bread bowl.

Mouthfeel

This is an asshole word meaning "texture." The only time people should ever be concerned with mouthfeel is when they are under the influence of narcotics.

Punishment: Suck on sandpaper and *then* tell us how your mouth feels.

Foam

Jesus weeps, I swear. These bubbles are nothing but food spittle. For all you know, there could be a station in the kitchen of assisted-living people sitting and chewing your dinner first and then dribbling all over your food. These are the things you need to consider when you see that on a menu, because any food that can create foam is either going to cause a disease or cure one.

Punishment: Being forced to eat any Hometown Buffet dish covered in its own foam.

"Two Ways"

How much Adderall are you on that you can't handle eating one piece of meat the same way *for the whole meal*? How about a hearty helping of *shut up* two ways? One with a disgusted look for the level of pomposity it takes to explain why you fried a piece of pork and then also roasted one, and another using my "finger feel" to determine which piece of meat is hotter so I know which one to throw at your face.

Punishment: Style Donald Trump's hair, because if you want to attain that level of tooldom, you need to understand the root of the word.

Coulis

This means jam. It means nothing but jam, except in Italy, where phonetically, it means "butts." Not so fancy now, is it?

Punishment: Having a dream in which Anthony Bourdain is allowed to do anything to you with a pork butt and you like it. The shame when you awake is paralyzing.

"BTBRTS" and "Sprinky Dink," both born of the criminally insane Anne Burrell

Okay, so in a way I like her because she has the gut of a Teamster and still insists on wearing sweaters. But I also realize that anyone capable of such atrocities as BTBRTS ("bring to boil; reduce to simmer") also has the power to kick out someone's teeth after two Long Island iced teas. I think this one is an arcing wire, the work of a madman. And so what if I can tell where her belly button is when she's wearing a turtleneck: "Sprinky Dink" is exactly what I would be doing out on the lawn after drinking two Long Island iced teas.

Punishment: Having your eyelids pinned open and being forced to watch Anne Burrell saying "Sprinky Dink" on a loop for one entire prime-time block while wearing a sweater three sizes too small.

"Y'all"

I just hate it, and it makes you sound fatter.

Punishment: For every offense, you must donate a toe to Paula Deen.

Sous-vide

Yeah. My mom used to use this cooking technique when she got her first job in the early eighties, called herself a "modern woman," and tossed almost every meal into a pot of hot water. We ate fowl, beef, and even some vegetables this way, but it had a different name back then. The English translation of *sous-vide* is "Banquet cooking bags" and if you ate dinner between 1975 and 1986, you are probably going to get cancer from it.

Punishment: Eat expired banquet "Tur-Qee" dinners bought at Grocery Outlet for ninety-nine cents apiece.

Gastrique

Or, in other words (such as the words that you use when you're not completely determined to impress somebody on the same level of jerkery as yourself), "sauce." Yes. *Sauce.* Simply sauce. If you really want to ruffle the feathers of the comment section, call it "gravy." Hee-hee. Gravy. *Gravy gravy gravy.* Although honestly, if you have ever been to the ocean on a superpolluted day and seen the bubbly, sometimes green, sometimes brown, always stinky residue that the waves have left on the beach and that looks like melted Styrofoam, I'd call that gastrique, too. Like what happens when the ocean farts.

Punishment: Say the word one hundred times in a row or drink a shot glass full of brown ocean foam.

Naomi Pomeroy

I honestly can't call who would win if Rachael Ray and Naomi Pomeroy were pitted against each other in an Annoy-Off. Can we just find a way to exile Naomi Pomeroy? She was the winner of *Big Fat Top Chef* or *Who's Afraid of Top Chef?* or whatever that show was called and is the proprietor of Beast in Portland, Oregon, and the woman simply cannot take a photograph without a dead pig slung over her shoulder. Google it.

That just says something about a person, doesn't it? If glaring at the camera with your dead eyes and consistently dissatisfied frowny puss isn't enough to get your message across, a dead farm animal should do the trick. Her finest moment, naturally, was when she was horrifyingly mean to her father, whose identity was concealed to her, on *Top Chef* as he tried to help her prepare a meal during a challenge. If you could be that awful to anyone who was trying to help you, you deserve to have that pig be the first thing you see every morning when you wake up. Plus, she charges $125 for a vegetarian dinner, and I don't think that includes a copy of the picture with the pig, either.

Punishment: Dress as Naomi Pomeroy shouldering a pig for Halloween.

Delish

If it's not something you would name your dog or if you're embarrassed to yell it out in front of strangers, we need to banish it from the *human language*. And there you have "delish." The first time I heard it, I was in high school and my friend who was in band tried to sell me a candy bar and that was her sales pitch: "It's delish." I shivered and declined, but bought one from a flute player in social studies who simply shrugged and said, "It's caramel and chocolate. I think."

"Delish" is one of those branding words that identify you instantly as one of those people who is so uncool that they actually tried to sell band candy instead of eating it all in their room and then stealing the money from a modern woman's wallet while she was sous-viding a pressed and sliced turkey in the same pot with broccoli drenched in a cheese gastrique.

Punishment: Sell band candy after you get fitted with braces. The old kind.

Savory

Holy shit. It just means salty. It just means salty and not sweet. It's just something you'd eat for lunch and not breakfast. That's all. Same difference between French toast and a grilled cheese sandwich. Savory = lunch. Mystery solved.

Punishment: Kick the next person who says it.

Gelée

What happens when the ocean eats dairy and its intestines shed their coating. Or, boiled and rendered horse hooves. Delish.

Punishment: A Jell-O hoof shot.

Bonus Round: Foodie

If you have ever used the word as a self-identifier in a sentence, have a T-shirt with it printed on it, or wrote it down without a smirk on your face or squirming in your chair, I'm sure you outsold everyone else in band during candy season. And guess what? We all eat food. We all like it. We all enjoy "the experience"; some of us just have more interesting things to brag about.

It's like breathing: it's everybody's game, but you don't see "Breathies" writing blogs about the exclusive oxygen someone flew in from France, or recounting how they inhaled some air that lichen can live in. Get a hobby. Develop a skill that takes more talent than just chewing and swallowing. Because you are really irritating.

And we all hate you.

HIERARCHY OF FOODIES

Every army has a pecking order, and the Amuse Douchers are no different. To rise in foodie rank, you have to be bold, you have to be fearless, and you have to . . . basically not have any other interests, hobbies, or loved ones who check in on a regular basis. We all suffer for our art, but with people like you around, we end up suffering for your art.

Here are the worst offenders, based solely on my experience with foodies who crush the boundaries of good taste—and they do it while they're popping capers with their teeth and talking about the versatility of sriracha. In order from highest to lowest, I present you with:

The Hierarchy of Foodies

We all chew, but they do it better than you.

The Lecturer

The guy who thinks he's Pliny the Elder and takes it upon himself to educate everyone at the table about the layers and nuances of each dish. Sometimes, when jealous, he will even stand up and wander over to your side to verify the accuracy of your assessment of the dish you ordered, are trying to eat, and will pay for. He will correct you when he senses you have erred, saying, "No, I'm afraid your palate is experiencing a user error. That was an atom-size particle of cumin I detected, not coriander." This guy also works in marketing at Wells Fargo, and after drinking a little, he tries to emulate the puddle of spit that gathers on the bottom of James Oseland's droopy bottom lip. He, at times, will hold up his hand during dinner, whip out his Moleskine notebook, and take notes while going for the big mouthfeel.

The Up-and-Comer

He has a list in his head (and probably hidden somewhere deep within his hard drive) of how many chefs know him by sight: "Chris Bianco waved back at me tonight. *Did you hear what I just said?*" "I know Matt from Matt's Big Breakfast. Used to be a bartender. Cool guy. Once, we talked about rosemary. Now he uses it in his breakfast potatoes. But I am cool with that." "In his studio apartment there is a collection of volcanic sea salt in a variety of earth-tone colors. One of them has the word 'clay' in the name. They are not to eat. They are simply to be admired. Looking only, please." The guy would draw from his sagging 401(k) if the right truffle came along. Just for the story, just for the legend.

MFA Fat Girl with Pink Hair

I am convinced there are at least seventeen copies of this same drone in a square mile radius of every city center, possibly dispatched from the Queen MFA Fat Girl with Pink Hair to cover more ground efficiently. She's at every opening. She's at every "Taste of," "Culinary Festival," "Ben and Jerry's Free Scoop Day," and "Chef's Night" event. She's also at museum openings, where you will find her by the tower of cake balls. She once considered applying for the Cordon Bleu, but decided she couldn't be on her feet for that long each day. Her marriage is on the rocks because her code writer of a husband has celiac disease and won't bend to the pressure. It's sad. But food's not. She'll write you a short story about it. She is also oblivious that the "edgy" expiration date for pink hair was in 1993.

Modern, Cutting-Edge Parents

You know, those parents who refuse to leave the baby at home and brag that their offspring's fist "chewables" were roasted beets and chevre. "Oh. Parsley *loves* arugula. *Loves.* Has since she was nine months old!" Babies don't belong anywhere in which the place setting includes two forks, and not just because they will throw the first one on the floor. You had a baby; now stay home with it. It's not cute; you're not progressive; it would have been better had you brought your dog instead of your baby. Because people like dogs. People don't like Baby Foodies. All you're really doing is showing us that two selfish assholes devoted their lives to raising another selfish asshole. As if we really needed more.

"Now, What I Would Have Done . . ."

Who likes to dissect the menu and alert all dining companions to its flaws and what he would have done differently—this, after a semester in culinary school, although his current job is cooking up burgers and fries for a place called Quackers. He TiVoed all episodes of *Top Chef* and refuses to delete them, "just in case." His favorite game is Guess What Shit I Just Put in Your Mouth, blindfolded; he likes it because he once guessed "offal" (the organs of an animal, such as the brains, spine, and stomach) right and a drunk girl clapped for him. His biggest nemesis is mayonnaise from a jar, and he once had a hissy fit in the condiment aisle at Whole Foods because passersby "just weren't getting how easy aioli is to make with a simple immersion blender."

The Food Slut

The recent enthusiastic college grad, now in PR, who is present at every new restaurant the night it opens, drinks the water, takes a bite, and then goes home and vomits it all up. The Veteran Food Slut just keeps the morsel of food tucked between an enamel-less molar and her hollow cheek, like a squirrel that can't wait to grab a napkin and find a dark corner. She weighs as much as a diabetic newborn, has been in party pictures in *free* magazines almost four times, and as an undergrad, she once dated a waiter at a place where someone was nominated for a regional James Beard Award, though she denied it in a press release (because he didn't win).

Wine Slusher

Thank heavens you are here to save me from a humiliating decision that will haunt me for years to come. I drank the wrong wine with the right food last night. I know, I know, it was on par with Sophie picking which one of her children would live, but sit down and take your spittoon with you. I know enough to drink fruit punch with McDonald's and go with limeade with Chick-fil-A, so I'm good. Besides, I'd rather pluck chin hairs than listen to you say "Do you get that? Are you getting that? The undertones are so primitive, *so dirty,* it's like drinking earth" one more time. Just go home and make your own wine labels. It's Three Buck Chuck under there, because if it was something better, you'd never cover it up, plus you haven't figured out how to make your own corks yet. I'm sure that will be covered on the "Fraudulent Vinter" in an upcoming blog entry.

Facebook Foodies

Their Facebook pages are entirely devoted to nothing but food pictures and detailed descriptions of what they have eaten for each of their three meals a day, and sometimes snacks if they happen upon a midday food fair or they've brought in banana-mallow cupcakes with lemon basil frosting for a coworker's birthday—not because they like the coworker; they actually hate the coworker, but are seizing the opportunity to impress everyone at the bodily injury claims department that when they talk about tweaking convention in the art of pastry, they *know* what they're talking about.

Hint to FF: Have you ever heard of editing? If you simply show, say, every tenth picture with a person in it aside from yourself, so many sins will be forgiven. Truly. But really, the honest truth is that people care as much about your morel mushroom, saffron, and farmer cheese omelet as they do about, well, you.

And I admit: I got blue eggs once from the farmer's market and took a picture of them. I did. But one of them had some weird poxlike calcium deposit on it, so there's your hook. File under "Oddities." I've taken pictures of my pot pies, too, but only because I estimated them to rise in excess of 1,200 calories apiece. And that's magnificent.

Also note: Posting pictures of half-eaten food is akin to displaying crime scene photos of a mutilated corpse. It stuns the appetite into an hours-long hibernation. Especially olive pits, even if the pit bowl is something ancient you pulled from the ground in rural Italy. Just so you know, everyone wants to defriend you, but keeps you either out of irritation or because they work with you.

The Journey Man

Seriously. If you go to Cambodia to discover the cuisine, all I really want to know about your trip is what kind of parasite you got, what part of your body it came out of, and what the chances are of me getting it in the United States. Because I am not going to Cambodia. I don't care about the herbs, the oils, the wafting scents, although I have to admit I am frightfully interested in the food poisoning you got every single time you went back to the same food stall that had no refrigeration method and the "fish fresh from the river" that you ate three times. PS: I wasn't in the Peace Corps, but even I know there are *no* fresh rivers in Cambodia, and if you want to eat fish that someone caught in the people's toilet, I hope your parents know someone at the embassy. Frankly, I wouldn't eat anything in a country that is still finding corpses in public places unless I had an autoclave with me and plenty of batteries. But, you know. There are certain states whose sewer systems are suspect, too. Mississippi. Alabama. Michigan. Arizona.

The Yelper

Yes, I know you have thirty people following your "reviews," including a guy from Spain, and you've even been the first to Yelp about three of them, but—and I'm sorry to say it—once you leave a review of 7-Eleven, you lose all credibility with me. The thrust and power of the soda fountain may be critical information to the same people who are upset that the store on Seventh Street carries Cool Ranch Doritos and not Spicy Sweet Chili Doritos, but hopefully, they'll remember to take their meds tomorrow.

The only things you really need to say on Yelp are if you found a hair in the food, if you saw a rat in the dining area, if you witnessed the cook touch his private place and handle your taco, or if you know a guy who knows the guy who once worked as the plumber who cleaned the grease trap and relayed that the kitchen was so disgusting that he "would never even drink a soda in a can from that place." If you know any of that intel, awesome. If not, I hate to say that your review of the state fair is probably not going to land you a gig at *Food & Wine*.

As for Your Shitty Food Blog . . .

I know your mom and girlfriend say it's cool, but your mom still feels guilty about drinking heavily before she knew *for sure* that she was pregnant, and your girlfriend makes dresses from used sheets she buys at Goodwill . . . so, well, there you go. To make it official, you got the name and URL of Your

Shitty Food Blog printed on a T-shirt from Zazzle, but are still waiting for a fan to buy one. Not yet, not yet.

I know I am the Destroyer of Dreams, but if there's one thing that people could possibly care less about than your pictures of what you ate today, it's your waxing and waning in accompanying long-winded copy in a bite-by-bite, first-person creative nonfiction narrative. Slap yourself for every time you say the word "seductive," pinch yourself for every time you use the verb "slather," and kindly ram a fork into your belly whenever the nonword "commingled" comes out of your mouth. The presence of the word "defiant" is about enough to make villagers tear you limb from limb like Montgomery Clift in *Suddenly, Last Summer,* and I, for one, would provide an alibi for each and every one of them.

AM I A BOOK SNOB?

Box set in English or Japanese?

Costco only has Sarah Palin's books in American!!

IQ84

Is that good? I've never been tested.

Having both on my shelf is like a literary IMAX experience. Had it in preorder for a year.

You have used the word "membrane" when describing the plot of a book.

A good book will always have just an eye on the cover. And the title in ALL CAPS.

A good book will always have the words "wife," "daughter," or "club" in the title. Oh, yeah. And "help."

I'll never read a book that

I'm sure it's impressive, though.

I don't believe in labels, anyway, but puffy covers have better sex.

When your last short story was rejected by McSweeney's, you

"Connective tissue" is considerably more accurate.

Vom.

You limit your book review on Amazon to

Wasn't reviewed in the NY Times by Salman Rushdie or someone from Spain.

Didn't get more than ** in People magazine

PS: I know I would not have been a racist in Alabama in the 1960s. I would not.

Filed for unemployment benefits, fully expecting to get them.

Were surprised because you thought everyone liked wizards.

13 graphs

13 characters

The thought of a Kindle

Is just another thing I can put polka dots on!

My book club

Wordplay: Murakami

Fills me with spine-snapping rage.

F*** you.

Wooooo!!! Drunk bitchez!!

Definitely start with Hard-Boiled Wonderland or don't start at all. Idiot.

I ordered that last time at Sushi Station and it smelled funny.

Full-on Book Asshole

Full-on Book Trash

DEATH CAB FOR COOTIES

*I*t looked like an ordinary yellow cab.

When it pulled up to the curb of the hotel in Cincinnati, no one fled from the backseat murmuring, "I'd get the next one if I were you," or shook his head at me like a pitcher shaking off a catcher. There were no warning signs, no caution tape stretched across the backseat, no body bag in the trunk beside my suitcase. But as soon as I settled into my seat and the bellhop closed the car door, I knew I was in for a very long ride.

There was a distinct scent inside the cab, one that made me choke back a dry heave. It reeked of bad thoughts, lingering regrets, and possibly a touch of human decomposition. It reminded me of the predominant reason I never went back to Girl Scouts camp. Cinnamon toast is awesome, but when you show a little girl the hole the pack leader's husband's just dug ten feet from camp and say "Form a polite line and do not stare," you have just provided a ten-year-old with a lifetime's worth of recurring night-terror material.

Because that incident occurred when my frontal cortex was still quite malleable, I now sit up in bed in the thickest of darkness at least once a week, panting like a fat dog on a beach, sweating like I had just raced Jen Lancaster for the last Twinkie on Earth (another recurring dream—she wins) and waking my husband up in the process.

"You had the dream?" he always asks, to which I nod.

"Train station or the Twinkie fight?"

"Train," I say as I nod again, but I still can't catch my breath.

"Just the toilet sitting out in the open?"

"Mmm-hmmm," I reply in a whisper, still seeing it as freshly as if I were still there. "No door. No walls. *Just a potty.*"

"And the Chinese lady who stands over you and yells, '*You take too long!*'?"

I nod my head again. "She's *so mean,*" I whimper, as my face collapses into that of a cranky toddler's.

"I know," my husband says soothingly. "I know."

I turn and barely say to him, "I just don't want to wipe," looking for understanding. "I just don't want to wipe."

And now, because I still think there are some soft spots

in parts of my brain, I was sure the smelly cab was going to translate into something far more paralyzing than an angry Chinese lady with a full bladder. It smelled like an open sewer—the odor was foul and aged, and the stench infested every crack and surface of the taxi, wrapping me in a gagging embrace.

It was too late to orchestrate an exit; I was on my way to the airport, my suitcase was in the trunk, and the driver, a husky man in his thirties, had already merged onto a highway. So I covered my mouth with my hand, pinched my nostrils as closed as I could bear, and tried to focus on anything besides the putrid stink sinking into every pore I had that wasn't already blocked with body cream from the T.J.Maxx clearance shelf. I cracked my window to let as much of the funk out, but the glass edged down an inch and then stopped, trapping me in the taxi tomb with its fetor.

The odor staunchly refused to move.

What could possibly smell so bad? I thought to myself as I surveyed the scenery, watching Ohio turn into Kentucky while I prayed for the airport exit to appear. What could be causing this foul odor? It *is* Kentucky, I reminded myself; maybe someone left a farm animal in the trunk a month ago after he got dropped off at his whiskey still? Could someone have shoved a diaper in between the seat cushions? Oh my God, am I sitting in someone else's muck? My friend

Andrea sat in homeless pee once on a bus in Denver. It made a great story, but no one really wants that in their repertoire. I quickly examined the seat and saw no kind of residue beneath me. Nothing. I was safe.

My mind raced, trying to solve the mystery. Surely, it can't just be the smell of the cab. I've even lost a milk shake in my car before during July in Arizona and it didn't smell this bad. Is it flatulence? It can't be, I reasoned, fully wanting to believe I was breathing in eau de diaper rather than eau de cabdriver exhaust. He would have had to hit six different countries in the last eight hours, including dropping by India to snatch up some curry off a questionable street cart and then drinking water from Mexico, in order to cause this level of intestinal distress. Anthony Bourdain has never eaten anything that could have resulted in this, even meals he watched die. I was at a loss.

Meanwhile, the smell was not abating; in fact, it was becoming thicker with every passing moment. Soon, I'd have no choice but to kick the window out or risk making my own contribution to this stinkhole. What the hell is going on in Cincinnati that no one has reported this criminal scent to the authorities? I wanted to yell. This was definitely a life-sentence-without-parole brand of smell, there was no doubt about that. Premeditated, indeed.

Just as I looked out the window and wished I could stick

my head out of it like my dog, I saw a sign for the airport. I had two miles to go. I can make it, I reassured myself, I *will* make it! I can hold my breath for two miles! If he goes sixty miles per hour and runs every red light, that's only two more minutes!

As the cabdriver took the exit, I saw the air traffic control tower on the horizon getting closer, closer, closer. I was almost free to breathe! Just then, the driver turned his head in my direction and asked, "Which airline are you at?"

I started to show four fingers in a misguided attempt to pantomime the words "US Airways" so that I wouldn't have to stop holding my breath. And it was precisely at that moment that I solved the mystery of the overwhelming stench.

It was his breath. That terrible, sickening smell was coming from his mouth. And the sickest part of it was that I knew I wasn't overreacting when the urge rose up inside of me to scream as if I suddenly had found myself sitting in the middle of Grand Central station with no pants on and a wad of Charmin in my hand. I quickly grabbed my purse, got my wallet, and rummaged through it to find enough cash for the fare so I wouldn't have to stay in that cab a second longer than necessary.

I grabbed a twenty just as the cab pulled up to the curb and stopped in front of the US Airways terminal. Just as I leaned forward to hand it to him, he opened the car door to get out.

I'm not exactly sure what happened next—I don't know whether the bottom of his nylon sweatpants caught the handle of the seat adjuster below, whether one foot stepped on the hem of the other pant leg, or whether the elastic suddenly around his waist had surrendered and exhaled its final, exhausted breath. I can't say. All I know is that as I leaned forward, I saw the shiny navy blue material bolt south, cresting over a wide expanse of flesh and gathering momentum for its last push to the bottom of the hill, and before I could shoot backward, the driver's exposed, unveiled ass was less than two feet from my face.

Without missing a beat, he immediately reached back, grabbed his waistband, and yanked it back over his enormous, bare, brandished posterior and slammed the cab door like it happened a million times. Every. Single. Day.

There are moments in life that pass all too quickly, and there are those that drag all too leisurely, siphoning every grain of time they have left in the frame. Then there are moments that make the world halt, that hold you hostage long enough for the comfort of denial to settle in, until you believe that a cabdriver's pants did not fall off at the distance from your face that you would normally hold an ice cream cone. This was one of those moments.

It was at this point that I wondered why it was that I stopped carrying a flask of bourbon in my purse. If you had asked me prior to this moment what circumstances would have allowed me to become nose to cheek with a stranger's bare buttock, I only could have surmised that I had become a crack whore, and even then, I would not be the one about to hand over a twenty-dollar bill. Especially not to a stranger who couldn't be bothered to brush his teeth for decades, let alone secure his danglies with some undergarments.

I will admit that I held back on my typical twenty percent, but do believe that some solid advice can take the place of monetary gains when administered properly.

"Here's the fare," I said, finally relinquishing the twenty as I fled from the cab. As I grabbed the handle of my suitcase from him, I took a large step back, looked him dead in the mouth, and said: "And here's a tip: Whatever about the dental floss, you've got three teeth left, you'd just be going through the motions at this point. I get it. But before other parts of you start to rot, too, you need to buy some goddamn underwear."

But what I didn't see coming was his jaw dropping just as quickly as his pants. Within seconds, his concentrated fetid breath shot in a direct line out of his mouth and into my sinus cavity, where the scent firmly planted itself and remained until I reached my gate and headed into the two thousand miles of airspace beyond.

THE RED CHAIR

It was the grandest red chair I had ever seen.

I couldn't believe my eyes.

The contour of its winged back flared out at precise, perfect angles; the brass tacks flawlessly aligned along the edges of the armrests fixed the dark, deep red bouclé upholstery firmly in place; the arms rolled outward slightly in an invitingly wide curve, as if going too far in one direction would be unforgivable.

I loved this chair.

But it was too late. I had already pledged my allegiance to the antique dressing table that was displayed in the window of St. Vinnie's, my favorite thrift store. I had unabashedly lusted for a three-mirror table for most of my adult life, and I couldn't have found a more perfect one than if I had rubbed my own belly and made a wish. The cashier had my debit card and a SOLD sticker was slapped on one of the mirrored panels before I even looked over and saw the glorious chair. And the side tables that matched the vanity. And the antique footstool covered in floral, cabbage rose chintz. And the incredible floor lamp, and the carved rocker, and the overstuffed settee in white linen. But the standout, I felt by far, was the chair.

"How much is that?" I asked without a second's hesitation, knowing full well that if he said anything below sixty bucks, I was going to take it even though I knew that I was already going to have trouble sneaking a dressing table into the house, never mind a huge 1930s wingback chair.

"It's $74.99," the cashier said without looking up, and handed me the receipt for the table.

"Oh," I scoffed, more grateful than anything that I had just escaped the trap I had set for myself. "That's far too much. Far too much."

The cashier shrugged.

"It's too much," I said in a whisper and I nodded. "It is."

"Okay . . ." the cashier replied.

Fine, I thought in my head. *Charge too much for a red chair. See if anyone will buy it! I thought you were a charity! Shame on you for letting people go hungry or naked or whatever because you priced a chair too high!*

But as I was leaving, I had to pass the red chair on my way out. I reached out and touched the wool upholstery, still in great condition, eyed the broad, wide expanse of the seat, the sweeping curves that flared out with elegance of a bygone era. "Oh," I heard myself whisper, "I love you. How I do!"

It was the Great Gatsby of chairs. Understated yet bold, subtle though demanding. A classic. A standard set so high that other chairs wilted in its shadow, afraid, lesser. I pictured it in my living room, layered in newspapers and unopened mail. In my office, with my computer perched in its lap. In my bedroom, smothered under an enormous pile of wrinkled clothes.

I could not bring this chair home with me, I told myself; I could not. I find it very difficult to pass up once-in-a-lifetime deals and they happen all the time to me. As a result, I already have two Victorian couches, an antique architect's desk, a steamer trunk, and an eighteenth-century French pine door in my subterranean wing, which is what I like to call our basement.

However, I have plans for everything, and I keep telling my husband this. I will get to the couches as soon as I master the art of reupholstery, which I will probably start sometime in my fifties, possibly sixties; the desk will go into the library as soon as I marry my second husband (hopefully a plumber), who will make enough money to build one; and I will use the door when I buy a house that is missing one that measures nine feet tall.

And I know danger lingers right around the corner. I am aware of that. I'd be lying if I didn't admit that I do have true concerns about becoming not just a hoarder but a hoarder who goes down in hoarding history, like the Collyer brothers, who died in their New York City town house when one of the brothers—while attempting to feed the other brother, who was blind and immobile—was crushed by his own booby trap of newspaper bundles and a baby carriage to catch "intruders"; as a consequence the other brother starved to death ten feet away . . . although their bodies were found two weeks apart. Or Big and Little Edie Beale of Grey Gardens, who had a twenty-eight-room mansion but used only three rooms because of the abundance of trash, raccoons, and cats that ruled the rest of it. Or Howard Hughes, who held on to his urine and collection of fingernail clippings for far longer than was really necessary. My husband shares these concerns and is convinced he's going to die in a fire fueled by my abundance of ephemera, with his major lament being, "People will never know that I was funny."

So when I came home with the announcement that my lifelong quest for the perfect dressing table had just been completed, he was far less thrilled than I was.

"Great," he said without looking at me. "One more place you can put paper in."

"It's an awesome table," I said. "It's got a three-way mirror and rosette carvings on the front."

"Where is it going to fit?" he asked. "In between the two Victorian sofas in the dungeon where it can get nice and warped and grow mushrooms on its legs? Does it even fit in the bedroom?"

"Yes!" I lied. "I just need to move the pile of clothes that need to be dry-cleaned over to where the pile of clothes that need to be lint rolled is, and put the piles of clothes that are moth-eaten or have stains I can't get out into the plastic bins, so I can put those in the basement until I decide I can't save them and then throw them away in roughly twelve years' time."

"You should have been an engineer," he said, starting to walk out of the room.

"One more thing," I said, standing on my toes in unbridled excitement. "There's this red chai—"

"No," he said as he walked into the kitchen.

"But you don't understand," I said, presenting my case. "It's magnificent and—"

"No," he said finally, without even turning around.

Okay, I thought. *I get the hint. I have pushed the limits with the vanity, I need to back off and let it go and forget about the chair.*

For dinner, I made his favorite meal and tried again after he took the first bite.

"This is great," he said, giving me the nod of approval.

"It really isn't great," I replied. "There are very few things in the world that are great, like Ben and Jerry's Chocolate Therapy, Yo-Yo Ma, Gandhi, and the red chair. That's how awesome the red chair is."

He didn't say a word. He didn't even look at me.

"As I was trying to explain earlier, I was at St. Vinnie's when I saw the vanity, and then the red chair—"

"Stop with the red chair," he advised. "I'm never going to say yes. We have too much furniture in this house as it is."

"But you don't understand," I pushed. "It was incredible in there. Somebody *really good* died, because it was like walking into my own estate sale. There was stuff that seemed like it already belonged to me. So it's like I have to get it back."

"This argument would have much more weight if you didn't meet an eighty-year-old lady with crazy hair, wearing bright red glasses and a beret—at a jaunty angle—with a huge red velvet flower on it while walking the dog last week and become convinced you just met yourself from the future," he added.

"I'm sorry," I said adamantly. "That was future Laurie, and you are in for a wild ride, my friend!"

"If you say one more word, I'm going to tape you and play it for people," he informed me.

The next day, I woke up from my dream about sitting in the red chair, in which I was wearing my favorite lint-free smallest dress from 2000, eating Ben & Jerry's Chocolate Therapy, and my bald spot (I reserve the right to call it a cowlick) had almost completely grown in.

An hour later I repeated what I could of the dream and realized that unless I had arrived already equipped with ice cream, I was foolish to even try. Every St. Vinnie's employee who passed offered to help, to which I replied that being in the store "was like being at my own estate sale. Somebody *really good* died!" until the manager came over and told me he'd give me a discount if I'd sit in that chair all day—at my own house:

"Ten dollars off," he said.

"Fifteen," I volleyed.

"Sure," he answered. "Sixty and the chair is yours."

"Will you hold that price for twenty-four hours?" I bargained. "In the meantime, I want this rug. It looks very familiar to me. Like I've walked on it before."

I was dragging the wool rug into my house when my husband came home early.

"What are you doing?" he asked as I struggled with the small fifty-pound, bedroom-size rug.

He looked at me and when I didn't say anything, he shook his head.

"Did you buy that at your estate sale?" he asked.

"I was just visiting the red chair," I tried to explain. "And I saw this."

"I thought we were past the red chair," he said. "I thought that was your obsession for yesterday."

"I got him to come down on the price," I said weakly with a trace of hope. "It's only sixty dollars now."

"I'm never going to say yes," my husband reminded me. "Never."

"I'm feeding hungry families," I added. "Or naked ones. Probably both at the same time. And they only need the price of a cup of coffee a day to live well. I don't know if that's deli or Starbucks prices, but the point is I am making a difference." My husband looked at me expressionlessly, waiting for me to finish. "It's for the children. They're naked," I added.

"We don't need another chair," my husband said. "There are nothing but chairs in the living room as it is. You don't even sit in the leather chair you bought at St. Vinnie's two months ago. It looks like Rent-A-Center in here. All we need is a couple of washing machines and we're set!"

I didn't say anything else about the red chair. Not through dinner, not during commercials that my husband forgot to fast-forward through when we were watching TV, not when we were playing with our dog. I waited until he put his sleep apnea mask on, a complicated facial contraption/vacuum apparatus complete with buckles, snaps, and an accordion hose that rises from the middle of it and stretches out about the length of an intestine. I am positive that in the fire that will ultimately engulf us, my husband will squander his chance to live because he'll be too afraid to run outside and let another man see that he had let his wife browbeat him about his snoring until he agreed to vacuum-seal an elephant's trunk to his face for eight hours a day.

With the whir of the machine going, I climbed into bed and faced the red chair's greatest adversary.

"Hey," I whispered right into his face. "I know what I could do with the red chair."

My husband's sleepy hand batted me away like a pesky mosquito.

"I'll use it in my office for my sewing chair," I continued. "Can I get it?"

His mouth opened and made a huge sucking noise, which I understood as "Yes, you must go and fetch the red chair before another lucky husband gets to have it blocking doorways in his house."

After I woke up in the morning, I immediately showered and squealed into the St. Vinnie's parking lot. Within fifteen minutes, I was back in my driveway with a red chair sticking out of the hatchback. I dragged it into the backyard next to a dresser I forgot I bought at Goodwill. I wasn't hiding the chair exactly, but I knew it was a sore subject and didn't want to make it worse by flaunting it so soon.

The next day, my husband was taking out the garbage, bumped into the chair, said "Ow," and continued on his way without a word. He said nothing. I breathed a sigh of relief—his initial confrontation with the chair had come and gone with not so much as a dirty look in my direction. I took that as a very good sign that although all was not exactly well, I'd overcome the first hurdle in getting the chair onto the premises undetected. Still, I was hesitant to press my luck and move the chair into the house. I figured by the end of the week, he'd be used to hurting himself on it and I could complete the relocation.

The next day we were sitting on the deck when he looked at me and said, "I'm so glad you let that red chair thing go. You haven't said a word about it for days and I really appreciate your considering my opinion on it. I'm sure it found a good home."

My eyes got wide. I smiled. And I panicked a little.

"I think it did," I said. "Once I get it inside."

He shot me an incredulous look.

"You said I could get the chair! So I did! It's under the

deck. It is ten feet from you. And you ran into it yesterday!"

"I did not," he replied, quite adamant.

"Look at your knee! I bet you have a red chair bruise on it," I added. "You would be the worst witness ever to take the stand."

"Eyewitness testimony is notoriously unreliable," he informed me. "What shirt was I wearing five minutes ago?"

My mind went blank. I didn't know. I was stumped. What *was* he wearing five minutes ago? I had no idea.

His smile grew bigger as my silence did, and then I took a chance.

"I have an answer, but if I'm right, you have to help me move the chair into the house," I said, to which he nodded.

I pointed at his chest. "You were wearing that shirt," I said, knowing that in our house, once we get dressed, that's pretty much it. We could have a carotid artery splash like a fire hose on our clothing and we would seriously weigh the effort of finding another clean outfit or just ignoring it until bedtime required otherwise.

He laughed. And then he helped me bring the chair inside.

I promised not to go to St. Vinnie's anymore, in addition to promising that I wouldn't buy any more furniture from Goodwill or Value Village, or bring anything home that I found in an alley. Later that night, when I passed by the living room to go to the kitchen, I saw my husband reading a book.

I'm sure that he abandoned the effort of getting to the couch after trying to scale the valley of the red chair and realizing he would need some rope, a spotter, and something to pee in, but that really didn't matter. He was relaxing in the chair, with its wingback so widely and elegantly spread, the brass tacks in perfect, gleaming lines down the sides, completely blocking the doorway from the living room to the dining room.

It fit perfectly.

I'M GONNA GET YOU

$\mathcal{L}$ast week, I was on a flight from Salt Lake City to Austin to visit some friends, and the man seated next to me, who had not uttered one solitary word for the whole hour we had been in each other's breathing space, suddenly flipped off his seat belt and ran down the aisle toward the cockpit. It happened immediately after beverage service, so I told myself he must have had to urinate superbad. So bad that he didn't care that he looked like Mohamed Atta as he catapulted out of his seat. His enormous body was so large that he had to sit sideways in his seat merely to fit, but he was surprisingly fast.

The need to pee is a powerful motivator; it can rouse you from a wonderful dream in which you are carelessly digging into a ten-pound slice of cake from Cheesecake Factory by yourself; it can drag you away from the last fifteen minutes of *Inception;* and it can force you to put the responsibility of ordering dessert in the hands of your husband, who once misheard the words "Can you get me the bananas Foster?" as "I'll just meet you out in the car."

Despite his suspiciously terrorist behavior, he would not have been the person of interest I would have picked out of the security line. First of all, his physique did not lend itself to jumping over hurdles, eating nothing but roasted goat, and living in caves in Pakistan, which is where Sara Rue and Jennifer Hudson secretly have been. He also had a neck tattoo of the sun, a clear lapse in judgment that would make any al-Qaeda leader wary of putting him in charge of the dirty bomb.

Then again, it's always the ones you least expect; I've watched enough *Scooby-Doo* in my life to know that much. Still, I gave the guy the benefit of the doubt and took advantage of the elbow room, only to have the flight attendant take his seat twenty minutes later, lean over, and ask me in a whisper what I could tell her about the man who had been sitting there.

After I told her that I didn't know him, she replied that he had told her that when he was in SLC, he got involved in some drugs, and now "the dealers were sitting all around him and were out to get him." I glanced at the two cute boys with spiky hair in front of me, who were taking turns sleeping on each other's shoulder—drug traffickers rarely kiss each other, so we could rule them out. And if the woman across the aisle was selling meth bags, she was really good at acting like she was enjoying every smug word of *Eat, Pray, Love* while unabashedly picking at the dead skin on the soles of her bare feet. And the middle-aged man behind us was clearly too busy trying to hit on the hottie half his age seated beside him to sell a gram of anything.

And I, by the way, was eating the complimentary biscotti and trying to conjure enough turbulence with my mind power (yes, even people who still have nightmares about fractions can have mind power) to coerce my seatmate's untouched biscotti to slide off his tray and into my purse. So, obviously I couldn't have been pushing pills on him—it would take way too much mind power for someone who still has nightmares about fractions to sell drugs *and* coax those cookies into my purse.

As a result of his paranoid complaints to the flight attendant, the purser thought it was in the best interest of the remaining passengers that he be seated up front, away from the girl in 17D with the fat ass and arthritic knees who was too busy eating her in-flight biscotti to realize that her enormous seatmate was losing his shit at a cruising altitude of thirty thousand feet. Either that or it was all a ruse to move closer to the cockpit so he wouldn't have to run as far in his flaming underwear.

The flight attendant then went on to tell me that the authorities would be meeting our plane at the gate, but if the Big Ray of Neck Sunshine returned, I was to alert her immediately. Which, honestly, took a little bit of the enjoyment out of the last bite of my cookie. But I did feel a bit relieved that if my seatmate returned with a knife in one hand and a nice bottle of Chianti in the other, this 110-pound blonde in a size 00 pantsuit would come to my rescue in her Christian Louboutin knockoffs from JCPenney.

I was going to ask her if she could drop off a few more biscotti, you know, because I am always far less nervous when I am chewing. But I thought better of it in the end lest she think I wasn't taking the situation seriously enough. Which couldn't be farther from the truth. In fact, I take any kind of erratic behavior on airplanes very seriously—doesn't matter if it's coming from terrorists, schizophrenics, or children. When I see the wheels popping off the bus, I am not afraid to press that stewardess button.

Which is why I need to find investors for my multimillion-dollar idea: Batshit Airlines—the go-to airline for anyone who doesn't take his lithium or haloperidol on a regular basis. Passengers are strapped into straitjackets, outfitted with noise-canceling headphones, and tuned into the guided relaxation channel until the captain turns off the restraints sign. At that time, flight attendants will come through the cabin, dispensing sedatives and electroshock treatments as needed, and—for an extra charge of seven dollars, payable by credit card only—a variety of pills are available for recreational use, all of which can be found at the back of your in-flight magazine.

Batshit Airlines may sound elitist to you; it may sound like I am trying to round up all the nutjobs so as to keep "their kind" off commercial flights (even though I would obviously say it was "for security reasons"). And if that makes me elitist, then call me Sir Richard Branson, because if I have to stand in line to have my ass crack x-rayed to see whether I've got a stick of dynamite tucked in there, I should at least have a say in who will be sharing my recycled air.

Passengers would just have to answer a few questions, like: "Have you ever slaughtered a family pet?" or "What's the last thing you've seen shape-shift?" A couple of brain scans of the frontal lobe at the security checkpoint for good measure and you'll be cleared for takeoff. Batshit Airlines also features a separate security line for entitled mothers too cheap to buy their devil spawn their own seats and too lazy to discipline them when they get loud and spastic. If these toddlers have enough endurance to kick the back of my seat for two hours and nine minutes, they can handle any ass-hole who's just snorted bath salts and tried to eat a homeless person naked.

Maybe it's an unpopular position, but I really don't want to fly the friendly skies with anyone who looks like a character on *True Blood*. I have enough of an issue with that nutjob standing behind me in line at Safeway, the one buying duct tape and a case of Capri Suns who smells like a gigantic wheel of ripened cheese. I certainly don't want to be within Bad Touch reach of a lunatic, let alone a guy whose psychotic ass fat is grazing mine. I don't need the extra stimulus. Seriously. Pave another road with it. I have enough anxiety worrying about the air-blowy machine coating me in germs. I don't need the additional stress of flying over the cuckoo's nest with Chief boxing me in.

Batshit Airlines: Where Most of the Turbulence Is Your Brain Chemistry.

SINS OF THE PIN

*L*ook away! Look away! Why can't I look away?

Every day, I cringe. Every day, I gag. And yet I continue to visit Pinterest every day, and every day I witness atrocious food pins signaling the demise of a society that is crumbling around its very foundation. True, I've scored some great ideas and recipes on the site, but more times than not, I'm trying to control my gag reflex when it comes to seeing what people find acceptable to share in public. But isn't.

Take this as a gentle guideline, a subtle suggestion, or an innocent approach to navigating the malignant waters of the pinning ocean. If I thought this trend would sputter and fade within a reasonable amount of time, I wouldn't bother even mentioning it, but I'm afraid that this has all the hallmarks of a virus that has the potential to mutate and jump species.

Twenty years from now, legally, you might not be able to make a sandwich without a tutorial and photos from six angles. If you want to live in a world where a Milky Way Midnight bar has no choice but to come complete with the crunch of chia seeds, keep pinning, people. Otherwise, take heed.

Here are six signs that Pinterest food pins are destroying the world.

6. Unconventional food vessels. I don't know how many mason jars you have hanging around your house, but if you don't have a farm and the answer is more than five, it's time for a garage sale, my friend. Because hoarding doesn't happen overnight—it worsens over time like Madonna's music. A guy up the street from us was actually on an episode of *Hoarders* because he kept living in his hovel even after most of it burned down. He threw a couple of tarps over what was left of the roof and used a chain saw to cut out some new windows in the plywood with a sign that read CONDEMNED stapled to it.

If you were to ask his relatives, I'm sure they would say that mason jars were the first sign of trouble, and that it all started when he had a dinner party and thought it would be cute to serve individual salads in them. *Get it? Get it? You shake it!!* Containers of any kind are a gateway purchase on the road to hoarder.

So when I see a girl in a sequined headband buying twenty-four clay flowerpots at Home Depot with the intention of baking cupcakes in them, a range of emotions washes over me. The thing is, chances are the people who would put anything in a _____ (insert Pinny phrase here: "So cute!" "Yes please!" and "I'm going to do this!") jar, muffin pan, or test tube are the same people who put up signs asking you to take your shoes off before you walk through their house. Life is short. Skip the clay pots and use a friggin' plate.

(Full disclosure: In the interest of dissuading overachieving bakers wearing polka-dot aprons from sending strongly worded letters on adorable stationery to the publisher, or hoarders from stink-bombing my Facebook page with offended comments, let it be known that I have enough mason jars for a cameo on *Hoarders*. And I am throwing stones at every glass house on the block.)

5. Quinoa. Possibly the most annoying foodstuff to trend this year—even more annoying than the word "trend": quinoa. Please. I'm begging Pinterest. Can we stop with the quinoa, made even more annoying by the pronunciation of "kee-no-ah!!!" (Yes, the three exclamation points are correct, as is opening your mouth as widely as possible on each syllable.)

I'll be honest with you, I can't figure out what the hell it is. Is it rice, is it pasta? And really, who cares because it looks like larvae no matter how you cook it. Really. No matter how you try to convince me how delicious it is, I know it's not and that you are lying because you don't want to feel gullible alone.

If I'm ever in the jungle with flesh-eating bacteria rotting my limbs off and cannibals chasing me, I might eat it because I'm sure I'd find some under a fallen log while dodging my pursuers. But until then, back off, People of Quinoa. And for the sake of all that's holy, I am begging all hippies to stop putting it in brownies and making "mac and cheese" with it. I don't want to see another picture of bug-egg burgers or unhatched kale cakes. Enough is enough. Just because you saw it in the *Fearless Flyer* at Trader Joe's doesn't make it right.

4. Crock-Pots. I keep waiting for the wave to crest just like it did in 1984, when my mom finally unplugged hers and put it in storage, but all of the pictures of breakfast casseroles and creamy chicken thingies are making me believe in parallel universes and I'm stuck in the bad-food one. Almost every time I gag while on Pinterest, it's due to a slow cooker–induced wave of nausea. No more pizza casseroles, I beg of you. Stop making cheesecakes in them, or any recipe with the word "ranch" in the name for that matter. ("Ranch" is the word that often triggers my Crock-Pot gagging. Honestly, it works every time, especially when combined with the word "bacon.")

And guess what? Sure, you can make a sub sandwich in the slow cooker (I've seen pictures!), but it should take you eight hours to put ham on bread only if you have two hook hands. And hardly anyone has that. Guess what? I'm making chicken and dumplings right now. Without a slow cooker. I put the chicken in a pot—yes, a regular, metal pot!—and . . . turned on the burner. That was all. Yes, you can do it, too. *You can.* I promise.

Walk away. Crock-Pot recruiters have cast a wide net and are gaining influence across the country. I know the Mormon Church is giving one slow cooker away with every conversion, and yes, that's better than baptizing Anne Frank, but not much. Not really.

3. Cute eggs. I know it's simply a seasonal annoyance, but it really can't be over soon enough. Sure, I admit that the first time I saw a deviled egg with sliced green olives for eyes and carrot slivers for feet, I smiled. But much like anything you've seen 1,953 times in a single day, it becomes irritating and loses its festivity around the 500 mark—that's when they become sinister-looking, with those red irises and orange claw feet and that chalky yellow mush teeming with heart-stopping cholesterol. Should people continue to pin cute eggs, I believe that they should be required to show the mother hen what they've done. Not only did they eat her baby, but they humiliated it by making it into an olive-eyed, carrot-clawed facsimile of itself, if it had lived.

2. Artificial colors in anything edible. How bad do you want cancer? Bad enough to eat a rainbow of it? Personally, I think the red cancer would be the worst, but anything you swallow with artificial hues in it is going to pop a tumor out of your body the day after you eat it. I don't care if it's cake, a Jell-O shot, or a handful of Skittles, you're going to get cancer. I'm betting the pastel strain wouldn't be all that serious, hopefully an organ you have in multiples, but fire down any foodstuff dyed devil red or sunshine yellow and you might as well schedule a biopsy as soon as you swallow.

1. Artistic kids' meals. Um, apparently, there are parents out there who spend their free time cutting sandwiches into the shape of sheep or molding brown rice balls into the shapes of bears, instead of saying to their kids, "This is a ham sandwich. It's in the shape of a sandwich. I'm not going to sit here and mold the film set of *Fantastic Mr. Fox* so I can get you to eat a carrot."

Aside from the lack of forethought involved in training

their kids to eat that way, they are also more than happy to share their creations with other parents to keep the cycle of abuse going. I saw one photo of a child's meal on Pinterest that was an elaborate re-creation of Hobbit Hill, complete with extensive carving, molding, and styling. I bet it took twice the amount of time to make it than it did to clean it up once the kid threw it on the floor.

I saw another one that was a nest, compiled with green fettuccine for grass, cherry tomatoes as eggs, and crackers cut out in the shape of birds. This is the work of an enabler, and I am already crying for the kid's future wife.

I'm not completely without my quirks when it comes to food. I can be picky and weird and if something looks like chocolate, even if it's on the floor, I'll pop it in my mouth before I even consider what brown things on the ground could feasibly be. I don't like my foods to touch each other, and I can't stand the smell of fish, let alone eat it, and that's a result of a mother who would look at my untouched plate, wait until I threw up, and then say simply, "Oh, no, you didn't like your flounder? I guess you'll find out every Friday that being hungry hurts."

But who hasn't been messed up by her parents in one way or another? Eventually, you get old enough and make peace with your past. I, however, cannot make peace with the future if the crisis is not averted. So keep serving dinners in your mason jars, complete with landscaping with quinoa mountains crowned by a sun of yellow cancer eggs slow-cooked in your Crock-Pot, go right ahead. In fifteen years, I'm sure it will be no surprise when restaurants that serve you a menu offering a filet mignon in the shape of a pony, bunny, or elephant start popping up. Served with a side of cloud potatoes.

HORNY

I didn't know what to think when he reached across the table and took my hand.

Yes, my gut instinct was alarm, not only because I was having lunch with my ex-boyfriend, but because he should have known me better than to try to hold my hand while I was trying to eat. We had dated many years ago and between us we'd had marriages, divorces, children, a bankruptcy, jobs, disagreements with the law, and a period spent on the lam since the time we spilt. (For the record, the job and a marriage were mine.)

People can change. Some people can anyway. I might have eventually become someone who would really enjoy the moment when a former flame, his forearms covered in paint droplets, reached for my hand. But I was trying to eat chips and guacamole with my hand at the time. I was hungry. And one of the primary jobs of either of my hands is to feed me, not be obstructed by a larger, rougher hand dappled with Navajo White that was blocking my access to the avocado trough.

Whatever. I've known this guy most of my life, I thought. *Give him your hand, Laurie—he's just trying to be sweet. He even told you that you were "holding up good for your age" when you came back from the ladies' room . . . despite the fact that he saw you from behind when you left the table, so we both knew that was a lie.*

But he's been through a lot, I remember, his marriage didn't turn out to be the hippie love fest he had hoped and he's raising his kids on his own. He got their mother pregnant while we were still dating, by the way, but I hold no grudges. I really don't. She was a better choice for him than I was, and I'm thankful that she was so easily fertile, which often happens with runaway teenagers. So really, it was a small concession to give him my hand. *The guacamole can wait a minute. It's a room-temperature dish,* I reasoned with myself. *Although I am seriously putting a time cap on this thing, and when my fajitas get here, it's every hand for itself.*

I smiled, thinking it was sort of sweet—you know, after all this time. It was really kind of cute. Ex-girlfriend, ex-boyfriend, moving a little further out of their youth, each with small creases at the corners of their eyes. They both wear glasses. She remembers when he used to spend sixty cents on a Taco Bell burrito for her, and in exchange, she would sit on the floor of the Baja buggy he constantly worked on because he never put in a passenger seat. She remembers going to some of his rehab classes with him because his probation officer said it would be a good idea. He remembers the way her earrings chimed when she turned her head. Yay! We're alive! We weren't Sid and Nancy after all!

Life, at times, has been magnificent and terrible to them both. And now, at their favorite restaurant on the side of the freeway, a place they used to eat when it was new, they are two old friends holding hands. But as it turns out, only one of the friends was thinking how sweet it was and how fun it was to remember the charm and golden glow of their youth, when she suddenly felt a finger curl up under her palm, giving her the universal middle-school signal that he wanted to do something nasty.

I pulled my hand away so fast I nearly smacked myself in the face with it. I was stunned by the fact that a bespectacled man with a receding hairline just made a seventh-grade movement for a conjugal act *in my hand*. Had anyone actually ever performed such a motion outside of junior high or a prison visiting room? I wondered. And he wasn't even drunk, I realized, wanting to shake my finger at him in shame and hiss, "*Watch it, Sid!*" I was about to comment on his unseemly behavior when my lunch arrived. Not a moment too soon. I was so stunned that I just sat there, staring at it as fajita steam wilted my hair, which had, I admit, held up pretty good for its age.

Once my hand was safely balled in a fist at the edge of the table, I decided that I needn't comment on his inappropriate behavior because the speed at which my hand had recoiled at the stroke of his meaty digit spoke for itself. I would just rather gloss over the incident than deliver a lecture to a man-child—especially when one of us was happily married. Most of the time. Except for the moments when she wished she had bought her husband a Sonic Super Ear for Christmas, since he went mysteriously and tragically deaf the day after they were married, with the exception of when an episode of *Law & Order* is on or he's having a beer with one of his friends in a crowded, noisy pub.

Now scented like a sweaty grilled onion, I tried to think of something else to say, so I asked about his family and listened while he filled me in on their lives and kept my hand on my side of the table and out of porn sign-language radius.

The remainder of the lunch was pleasant, we talked about old times and he caught me up on the latest news from people we used to know with whom I'd lost touch. I was beginning to forget about the finger misdemeanor; in fact, I'd already downgraded it to an infraction and chalked it up to a nervous moment. Maybe he didn't even mean to finger my palm. Maybe it was just a twitch, a sudden jerk, an involuntary profane gesture that grazed my palm when it wasn't supposed to and had no meaning at all aside from being a misfiring of human chemistry.

I began to feel embarrassed for myself about jumping to such conclusions, and was sorry that I had such a severe reaction. I should have been cooler about it. *People have weird body spasms all the time,* I scolded myself. *I mean, my foot suddenly kicks an inch on occasion as if a doctor were checking my reflexes. And my pinky sometimes wigs out and shakes as if it's trying to fake out the other fingers and make a break for it.*

I actually shook my head at myself, something that was not lost on my ex-boyfriend, who asked me what was wrong.

"Oh, nothing, nothing. I forgot to run an errand for my mom," I lied.

To make up for my failing judgment, I picked up the bill to clear my conscience and we headed out to the parking lot, parallel to a major freeway, making it a little more litter-strewn and noisy than it used to be.

"It was great to see you," I said, giving him a friendly hug when we reached his car.

"It was great to see you, too," he said, reciprocating the hug. "Give me a kiss!"

I leaned in and gave him a peck on the cheek.

"Come on! How long have I known you?" he asked, laughing. "*Laurie!* Give me one on the lips!"

I don't think the warning sirens at Fukushima Daiichi nuclear plant could have been louder.

Stop being so judgmental! Be cool! Be cool! my mind screamed. *You are going to hurt his feelings if you haven't already! Just get in there and make it quick. Fraction of a second and it's over and done with. One, two, three!*

Kissonthelips!

And then, on four, I knew that the flick of the digit was, in fact, a come-on, a trigger-finger porn move and not a nervous tic or a vitamin D deficiency. Because when someone tries to shove his tongue into your mouth by pushing through your priggish, tightly pursed lips, like a slug trying to press through a hairline crevice in a rock wall, the window of possibility quickly slams shut, or at least my window of possibility did.

Frankly, I did not know that I could move that fast. Based on the speed of my recoil alone I think I need to enter the Olympics in the "Revulsion" event.

"Hey!" I managed to cry in protest. "I'm married!"

And so my ex-boyfriend, after a moment of thinking, looked at me and said frankly, "I'm horny."

I'm horny. Really? Did you really just say that? You're horny? As a taxpaying adult, I have to say that no one has ever tried to French-kiss me uninvited in a dirty parking lot on the side of the freeway in at least a decade and a half. And I couldn't pinpoint the last time I heard that line, but now that I think of it, it was most likely uttered from the same lips that just tried to pry my mouth open like a can of Navajo White. And he wasn't even drunk!

What I should have said was, "How about you call my husband and tell him that?" But despite the early warning signal when my palm "got fingered," I was unprepared for the attempted slide into a very advanced *and dirty* first base.

"*I am married,*" I repeated. Then I lowered my voice and added indignantly, "*We have a dog together.*"

And honestly, if I were going to disrupt my dog's weekend for alternate custody, I would hope that it would not be for a guy whose lunch I just paid for.

Again.

So I left, and the first thing I did when I got into my car was call my sister and say, "Guess who just tried to kiss me like a hillbilly on a reality TV show?" And after that, I called my husband and started to tell him the whole story.

"*Stop,*" he said, even before I got to the "I'm horny" comment. "Just stop."

"I'm sorry," I said, rethinking my decision to bring it up. "I didn't mean to upset you."

"I just can't handle it," he replied. "He sounds so . . ."

I waited for the word.

Infatuated?

Covetous?

Obsessed?

His pause spoke volumes. It was telling me: "You are a powerful woman. I don't know if you realize this, but men can barely resist you. That poor, consumed fool."

". . . *desperate,*" he finished.

Then it was my turn to pause.

"What?" I finally replied, deciding to give him a big dose of his own Sonic Super Ear medicine. "What? *I can't hear you!*"

SIX THINGS I NEVER WANT TO HEAR (AGAIN) WHILE STANDING IN LINE AT THE PHARMACY

$\mathcal{T}$here are certain places in a grocery store that are far more dangerous than others, and for the innocent, I'm not talking about the ice-cream aisle. I'm talking about the partitioned part where the Vicodin lives. True, if prehistoric birds attacked the store or there was a hostage situation, I'd always pick Pill Land over the candy lane as a spot to hole up. But in everyday, regular circumstances, it's a terrifying, naked place.

This leads me to admit that I'm there constantly because I cannot get my inhaler, my high blood pressure pills, and my Ambien dolls coordinated for the same pickup; as a result, I know everyone there on a first-name basis. You're not supposed to know the white-coats by name until you're about sixty-eight, but at least I'm ahead of schedule for *something*. Still, when I get the phone call reminding me that my prescription is ready to be picked up, I shudder.

If you really want to be afraid for mankind, you don't even need to know who Paul Ryan is. All you have to do is lurk for five minutes by the pharmacy.

Six Things I Never Want to Hear While Standing in Line at the Pharmacy. Again.

6. "Do you know where the stuff for lice is? Because I can't find it in the shampoo department."

I don't get it. Suddenly, kids have lice and everybody's cool with it to the point of broadcasting it in public. Did something happen since I was in school that has made these vermin an accepted part of childhood? I know bedbugs are all over the place, but lice? Really? Who keeps going to Eastern Europe and bringing this shit back? *Stop going to places that end in "-ia,"* you guys. *Stick with France. I mean it.* Besides, I thought we got rid of lice and polio in the same vaccine. And to shout it out in a pharmacy line? This is what I wanted to say to that lady, in no particular order:

- "You are dirty and you should be more ashamed."

- "Put a friggin' plastic bag and a rubber band over your head if you cannot afford a shower cap, because one will not be provided for you."

- "If there was ever an unquestionable reason for the Internet to exist, this is it."

- "If my head starts to get itchy and I find eggs on my scalp, I am going to sue you for public endangerment of a hypochondriac."

5. "Hi. I was wondering if you could tell me what a staph infection looks like."

Let it be known that the person who made this statement did not have a prescription and had just wandered over from handling some produce when she plopped a five-pound bag of russets on the counter and proceeded to embark on a fifteen-minute conversation that included other standout sentences, including, "Infection can burrow," "Is there a head?" and "Have you tried to pop it?"

Also let it be known that I don't know exactly what can kill a staph infection, but I did feel that time was of the essence. After picking up my Ambien, I went directly to the freezer section, where I held bags of frozen peas until my hands burned, and also refused to buy anything for a month at Safeway that hadn't been through some level of chemical processing and irradiation.

4. "I Wish I Could Show You."

It was this statement that made me wish that pharmacists were allowed to put out tip jars like baristas because they take way more shit than anyone seems to realize, including having to talk people down after they threaten to remove vital items of clothing, which is way worse than people complaining that the design on their mocha isn't fancy enough.

Anyway, in this instance, an old man in overalls had a "scaly patch" he wanted an opinion on, after confessing that he scratched himself so aggressively he bled. Despite his detailed description, the pharmacy tech, who I believe did nails at the mall up until the week before, kept shrugging and offered an unsatisfactory diagnosis by telling him to contact a physician and not ask a twenty-year-old girl who had no more of a background in skin diseases than did the kid stocking eggs. Fearing that an impasse had been reached, the overalled man expressed his desire to reveal the patch itself, an offer the tech firmly declined. Thank God.

3. "Smith. S-M-I-T-H. It's for Clozaril. An antipsychotic. *Would you hurry up, please!*"

Awesome. The meds no one can find behind the counter are for the guy in line ahead of me who has the most potential to snap my neck like Liam Neeson while I quickly pen a good-bye note to my family on the back of my credit card bill. Now, I'm not saying that there has to be an express window at the pharmacy for people just picking up some asthma medicine. But maybe there should be a window that is designated specifically for the needs of people who have magical powers like time travel and who take orders from their dog. That window could come equipped with a tranq gun and a net that drops from the ceiling. Barring that, I have learned to keep a low profile, so that my mother doesn't have to live the rest of her life with my credit card bill framed on her mantel, while telling people: "She was an idiot. She stayed in line for her sleeping pills. And she was paying twenty-two percent!"

2. "Go ahead. Call the cops. I have a prescription, and the cop already hassled us outside, anyway!"

This from the Bonnie and Clyde duo of tweakers who hopped around like the floor was lava and they both had a hot potato in their pants. Now, maybe my strategic skills are a little dull, but I think the last thing I'd offer as proof that my prescription was real and not scribbled on a stolen doctor's pad would be that I was already considered a person of interest by the authorities before I even got in the store.

I'm sure their appearance had nothing to do with it, being that the only difference between a zombie and a tweaker is that a zombie is usually eating something. This pair got in four fights in the ten minutes they were in front of me and then made up with each other by picking at their face scabs. I was sure that if either one of them farted, it would blow a chemical burn through my leg. I don't know if they ever got their drugs; they were, naturally, standing in the wrong line.

1. "Whoever was in the bathroom when I told you before is still in there, and now they're moaning."

Leave it to a lady who isn't confident in the quality of her undergarments to announce that someone either just got high, just had sex, or just had a heart attack in the restroom right next to the pharmacy. There is nothing that could make me step foot over that threshold. I've seen what comes out of there and that's enough of a deterrent for me. It was dirtier than the Chili's in Redding, California—and *that* is saying something.

Honestly, I've heard sounds emanating from behind that bathroom door that sounded as if a rodeo were under way and that whatever was trying to get away repeatedly kept escaping. Yes, it is true, I have a thing about germs, but that doesn't discount the severity of human debris that accumulates within that twenty square feet. Once, my husband, who had been deathly ill for eleven days, came into my office to tell me about the new season of *Portlandia,* and then he stopped and said, "I know you're not turning around because you think if you don't face me, you won't get my germs and they'll bounce off the back of your head. But I have protected you." I turned around slowly to see that he was wearing a napkin around his face like a bandit.

So yes, I hate gross bathrooms and this one was located right next to the pharmacy, which quite frankly surprised me for a supposedly sterile environment devoted to wellness. This particular john had seen so many unseemly acts, most of which would have required a forensics team to decipher had a lady with bladder-control issues not been jiggling the door handle repeatedly. The manager was still banging on the door when I left, but I didn't care. I was sure that they would get whoever it was out of there before it was time to come back the next day and pick up something else.

I ONLY WANT TO KNOW
IF YOU HAVE HERPES

*I*f the Internet is the seventh circle of hell, as I believe it to be, then Facebook is without question its reigning five-star general. There's no doubt that the social network swamp is the first in the goose step, leading its troops into a swirling bottomless pit of cringes, things that cannot be unseen, and peeks at humanity that result in a creep factor worthy of Hieronymus Bosch.

We've all read our fair share of gasp-eliciting status updates from People You Thought Knew Better, but when it comes to setting the lowest common denominator, leave it to Facebook to repeatedly drop the bar. Again. And again. And again. It's rapidly becoming my go-to spot when my hope for mankind—which is composed of such highlights as seeing people wash their hands after going to the bathroom, the fact that Walmart hasn't run Target out of business yet, and those moments of kindness when strangers let me pet their puppies—completely flatlines and leaves me with a feeling of raw despair for roughly thirty seconds. Without fail, Facebook plants me firmly back in my place and reminds me that for every six-week-old Australian shepherd with a wagging tail, there's someone who can't wait to tell me that twelve people got killed in a movie theater because there's no prayer time in public schools.

The Five Creepiest Things I've Seen on Facebook This Week

5. Any relationship status identified as "open": Yeah, see, that's really none of my business. That is private information that you shouldn't be sharing, especially when you've been to my house for dinner. Thank God Facebook doesn't have an option to list your STD status, because I'm sure if you admit in public that your husband/boyfriend/sire of your illegitimate children is still very much swimming in the dating pool, I have no doubt that I would be wrestling with the news flash that you have genital herpes and have probably already sat on my toilet.

No, no, no. I'm not old-fashioned, you are. It's not the seventies anymore, so move on and get with the program.

Swingers are gross and it's not the same as sharing a soda with a friend on a hot day. It is not. Gross. I am grossed out. Now I have to look at you like you are a dirty person. Do you know what my mother would do if she knew I'd let you into my house? I'd never hear the end of it. "Oh, you want national health care for everybody? Sure, you and your swinger friends . . ." she would say.

So just keep your keys in your pocket, your diddling activity off Facebook, and do the right thing: alert me when the toilet seat needs a shot of bleach. That is something I definitely need to know, not that you can't close your eyes and use your imagination like everybody else in a dark room.

4. People who take photos of themselves and expose what a hovel their house is in the background: Hey! Nice cleavage! Is that your kid in the background? Awesome. Now uncross your arms, pull your shirt up, and wipe the macaroni and cheese off your wall that your offspring is licking.

Maybe I'm the only one who knows how to work a cropping and blurring tool, but if you're going to show every single person you know *plus some* what a truck stop your bathroom is, maybe you should walk through a tutorial or two. Or maybe do a quick sweep to make sure your panties and enormous Costco Kotex box aren't shining like pink beacons in the night.

Now, true, if you look at my profile picture, you are going to see a bottle of liquid fuel, a bunch of yarn, several open shoe boxes, a couple of Target bags hanging in midair, a red shoe lying alone on its side, a box of fabric that I still haven't unpacked—wait, make that two boxes of fabric that I haven't unpacked—and a bunch of torn pages from a magazine I tacked to a bulletin board that is partially obscured by the Target bags, but I consider all of that *set design*. And as I told the person who commented on it and begged me to let her come over and organize it, to clean up my office would be to destroy my world. I know where everything is. No one is allowed in here and I don't want anybody touching my stuff. I have my own system. *It works for me.* And at least my world doesn't let my coworkers and in-laws know I'm ovulating or that I buy maxipads in a box so big I have nowhere to put it but in my sink.

3. Any e-mail from a guy I don't know that begins with the salutation "Hey, Pretty Lady": Now, I'm not sure what it is I'm posting that is an open call for every lonely man from Pakistan to come knocking on my mailbox in search of transatlantic Facebook love, but I hardly think that a status update about finding little brown round things in my hair and believing them to be lice is a siren call. Then again, I don't know what is considered sexy there. I have no idea.

Maybe vermin scalp eggs are an attribute. I don't know, but I have to admit that it felt a little invasive, and my immediate thought was to shoot back an e-mail that said, "I just farted, Aqib. How pretty is that!" But then a smaller, quieter voice said, "Do you think he really means it?"

The thing of it is, Aqib, that I can tell you are very proud of your status as the richest man of your village, and I'm sure you worked hard to acquire your empire of three goats. However, I'm already the first wife here and you may be shocked to hear this, but I am running the show. I have no desire to become the Tuesday night appointment in your harem, and if I may speak frankly, I know you think you're rich, but I saw bin Laden's mansion on the news. It looked like Section 8 housing to me; in fact, it has a somewhat eerie resemblance to a block apartment building next to the freeway exit where crystal meth is openly traded in the parking lot like, say, kebabs. It was just as filthy on the inside, too, and he had a couple of wives. I know there was a tussle/bloodbath before those pictures were taken, but in all honesty that doesn't explain the filthy sheets on the beds. That rubbed patch of grime developed long before any Navy SEALs landed in that compound.

So I can imagine that any new girl on the block is going to be pulling the majority of that load, and I bet you don't have a stackable Whirlpool Duet, either. That is, I'm afraid, a deal breaker. I hate bending down. So, while I thank you, Aqib, for noticing my inner beauty, and there is much of it, I am going to have to pass on your offer. But may I suggest that you might have better luck finding a concubine if anyone is left over at MySpace.

PS: I know a couple of swingers; I can pass on your e-mail to them, too.

PSS: They weren't larvae eggs, but foxglove seeds after I knocked myself on the head with a spent stem, which I luckily realized before completing the plan of setting my hair on fire.

2. Receiving messages from the dead: I understand that Facebook is a little challenged in this department since you cannot entirely ever expunge your account (that may be something you want to fix, Mark), but I have to say that getting a friend suggestion from Uncle Dan, who died last summer, was a little more than unsettling. Sure, I respected his opinion, and clearly, we have several mutual friends already, but communicating with the beyond is a little out of my safety zone. I didn't set up a Ouija board, didn't hire a psychic, and I have no interest in setting up a portal to another dimension, so to hear from Uncle Dan unsolicited was, in a word, friggin' creepy.

If I am ever given the opportunity to communicate

with Uncle Dan in the unknown and ask some questions, they would be along the lines of "What did you do with my grandmother's wedding ring?" or "I was riffling through some old documents and I was just wondering if you ever got the feeling that Grandpa maybe wasn't your real father?" and probably not "Should I friend Shelley, the receptionist at your company who I have never met or spoken to?"

So yes, Facebook, please invent an "I'm Dead, Thanks," button so loved ones can truly rest in peace and not spend eternity haunting the right sidebar, still giving advice I don't want.

1. When someone else's profile is not of that person but of you: Initially, I thought it was curious that someone's profile looked so similar to my own; the style of hair, the position of the head, the expression on the face, until I looked close enough to see that the photo wasn't similar at all; it was exact. *It was me.* And where did I see this but on my own timeline, where the person who stole my face was leaving a comment on something I posted.

Now, this is altogether different from seeing someone who looks like you—this is a person who obviously went out of her way to swipe the photo, upload it onto her Facebook account, and select it as her profile pic, then flaunt it on my page. Who would steal someone else's head and claim it as her own? And why? The creep factor is mile high on this one, as I'd rather have Aqib and his open-relationship harem talk to my dead Uncle Dan in my office, eating Chick-fil-A, than see my picture popping up with someone else's name underneath. Again.

I kind of felt like I had been skinned, and that It had done a good job of spreading lotion on Its body. I didn't know what to do; I didn't want to engage a stalker, because any acknowledgment is pretty much an invitation to break into your house and wait around with some piano wire in hand until you get home. If you have any ideas on how to handle this aside from buying a pet lion, tell me.

The only other thing I can think of is to steal *her* profile picture and put it on my head. But I can't even do that because *it's already my head.* So if my real face goes missing anytime soon, the authorities will know to look for the *friend* wearing the Laurie hat on Facebook.

SPIT SWAP MEET

It was heading straight for my biscuits and gravy like an asteroid hurtling toward Earth. The arc was perfect. It shot into the air with impeccable form, a smooth, round curve gaining momentum with precisely perfect moment, bridging the span across the table with astonishing speed.

I was stunned, knowing that in the next moment, something gruesome was about to happen. In a flashback, I recounted the previous hours and the perfect afternoon my friend and I had before ducking into this trendy brunch place for a well-deserved and much-anticipated bite to eat. It had been a glorious afternoon. We stopped into a fabulous chocolate shop, where they plied us with full-size free samples, and when sweet and salt are combined, it's a known scientific fact that calories and fat grams are canceled out.

We saw the most glamorous old-lady alcoholic weaving her way down the street wearing leopard-skin hot pants, huge sunglasses, and the brightest red lipstick smeared over her puckered mouth and melting face, a mirror image of what her pillow must have looked like that morning. She was incredible, and she reminded us of what drunken glories our respective retirements could hold if we could just outrun cancer and diabetes a little bit longer.

And right outside the restaurant, we saw a gorgeous skinny girl crying, asking, "Why? Why?" to her brand-new ex-boyfriend, who was in the process of breaking up with her. And seriously, only a really good friend would know that after fake-reading the brunch menu posted in the front window, when you say, "I wonder if they have bacon here?" that you really mean, "Let's hang out here for a second until he answers that question or she blows a snot bubble."

So truly, it had been a day to remember, full of exceptional achievements and realized reveries (free chocolate, lady alcoholics in leopard skin, and sobbing models!), and not only had had our afternoon bonded us closer in only a way pure excess and evil can, but we also worked up an appetite while we were at it.

I was ravenous when we entered the restaurant and opened the menu with the delightful realization that of course I could order five pounds of French toast and a baker's dozen of biscuits and gravy, because a daily diet of chewing gum and five sips of Red Bull had done no favors for the girl now sitting on the curb with her protruding cheekbones in her skeleton hands that clearly no man wanted to hold. When our meals were finally delivered and my biscuits and gravy were placed before me, my mouth watered a little bit and I readied for the attack. I couldn't wait to dig in, and as I lifted my fork to go in for the kill, I saw *it* out of the corner of my eye, taking flight.

The tiny rocket of spittle launched from my friend's mouth as she was in the middle of telling me a story about a girl we knew who had been living in a run-down Winnebago that exploded after some illegal fireworks in it caught fire. My eyes followed it involuntarily as it entered the airspace on my side, then landed, skidding into the middle of my biscuits and gravy like a high jumper in a sandpit.

By the time I saw it, it was too late to cobble a defense together, even something as simple as attempting to swat it with my hand like it was a white fly or impure thought was out of the question. Seriously, even the most prepared person would be rendered helpless after realizing a drop of spit was charging at their food like a goat released from a medieval trebuchet, which had just landed with a barbaric splat! Really, I mean unless you're a character out of a trashy vampire book, no one has the lightning reflexes necessary to conquer such a juicy, hurried foe, but my reflexes were sharp enough to know that whatever beautiful promise of satisfaction and carb overdose my lunch once held, it was now lost to the ages, like Cher's real nose or American homeownership.

Gagging and covering your mouth is not a good move, so I'm sorry I did that, for two reasons: (a) retching noises with any amount of volume are never really welcome in a food service establishment and that becomes very obvious once you emit them; and (b) I then had to quickly think up a reason of what would trigger a such a reaction (aside from "Shit! You just spit all over my food!"), and saying you swallowed the cough drop you were saving under your tongue wasn't going to win you any court cases.

Also, mouthing the "F" word isn't particularly beneficial, either, and can cause hurt feelings, particularly if the Spitter knows what she's done and the defiled baked good now lies on the table between us like a dead possum. This can cause uncomfortable silence for the remainder of the time you spend together, which in my case was four hours, most of that being in my car. This will result in both of you feigning extended and painful excitement over the "performance" screen in a Prius, literally forcing you to make squealing noises every time it's noted that you're getting 99.9 miles to the gallon, which happens roughly every seven seconds, simply because there is nothing left to say except, "Have you thought about investing in one of those spittle-suctions they have at the dentist's office to suck up some of the excess saliva? Or perhaps a mouth sponge?"

After "the incident," I realized that if gagging was my go-to response, I was going to need to round it out with a believable finish to cover the fact that I found my dear friend's saliva so repulsive that it triggered one of the most undesirable physical reactions in the human repertoire. True, while gagging is far favorable to say, stabbing, the message is remarkably similar.

I could only hope that if I were on the precipice of a subsequent vomiting at the table in the same situation, I would not try to hide the fact, in hopes that my friend would hopefully ask if I was all right. (I must note here that this is not effective in the least with most husbands or sociopaths with an easily excitable parotid gland, and if you really want to avoid spittle flying on your food like a meteor shower, avoid dining with anyone on antipsychotic meds. I learned the suggested standard antipsychotic med radius of five to ten feet—depending on the visible froth—the hard way after hiring a guy with "emotional challenges" to clean the leaves out of my gutters. As he scrambled up the ladder, he relayed stories about his family—how his mother was a whore and that his father never loved her—and although I was transfixed, I was much more horrified to discover that those weren't raindrops I felt while holding the base of the ladder that day.)

Thinking quickly, I decided I'd try to trigger my friend's gag response by describing the *hair* I'd just seen in her biscuits and gravy. Should she be so bold as to investigate, I would just explain that: "*It was a thick hair. Heavy. It must have sunk into the gravy.*" And then . . . the coup de grace: "*It was curly.*"

If this is not enough to make her avert her eyes and hail the waiter, then either I am a worse liar than I thought or I need to make new friends. Unless you are someone who owns every single *Jackass* episode on DVD or you are a gynecologist or waxer, very few people could argue with having a gag reflex in response to that. And chances are, you've ruined their appetite as well.

Hey. They started it.

As my friend tried to get the waiter's attention to alert him to the "spoiled" food, I told her not to mention the hair and just have him bring two glasses of wine—each. After one brush with a saliva globule, I wasn't about to send the food back and risk the possibility of consuming a secretion from the cook's parotid gland.

I'd rather see a curly hair.

A HANDY MANUAL FOR
A WIDOWER, MY HUSBAND

After a close call with the Big Sleep yesterday, I am happy to report that I am a better person than I thought. Because when faced with the possibility of my own demise, my first thought was not to mourn my own passing; rather, I thought first of my husband. What would happen to him if I died? Yes, there would be a short period of mourning followed by a longer period of jubilation and buoyant celebration of his newfound freedom, but what exactly does that freedom mean?

It means that my husband would be left to supervise himself. And for a man who kept eating mystery cheese from the refrigerator until it actively burned his tongue (and never established that it actually was cheese), he might as well just be buried with me like in ancient Egypt. It would just be a matter of days until the backhoe was needed again. Therefore, with the help of several of my longtime married girlfriends, I have created "A Handy Manual for a Widower, My Husband." Feel free to annotate this list with your own individual inspirations.

Dear Husband,

If you're reading this, the inevitable has happened. I've stuck a knife into the old toaster you told me not to buy, which shot sparks at the dish towel you said I keep too close to the stove, and then burst into flames, igniting one of the expired coupons sticking out of that drawer that you enjoyed reminding me to clean out, before spreading to the rest of the house and killing me because I'm on Ambien, which you told me to stop taking because I was getting too "aggressive with my snacks in bed." Well, you don't have to worry about snorting Cheetos dust anymore in your sleep. You have found this note because I am dead, "death by misadventure," and you are finally going through the motions of rifling through my things so you can throw it all away, because I'm guessing your new lady friend requires some additional space in, well, my house. *Not so fast,* my friend. I have a couple of words of advice for you.

You may not know it, but take it from me, a dead person, that your mortality is as fragile as a piece of cheese bread that has fallen apart in an electrical appliance. First, a few commonsense things that you probably already know, but a dead wife has to cover all the bases to rest in peace:

1. Never put a fountain in the front yard unless you just joined the mob.

2. When your next wife has a birthday, it is not enough to invite people to a party. You actually have to throw one.

3. Do not let your second wife wear my clothes.

4. Go back out to the garage and move my goddamn clothes back into the house. Now.

5. Never do your Heidi Klum impression out of this house. No one will ever get it when you say "That dress makes me sad," and it sends an otherwise terrifying message. You sound like you swallowed a chunk of banana whole and are about to throw two small children into an oven.

6. Bring your sleep apnea machine with you on dates. Yes, I know showing up with a suitcase full of medical

equipment might be a deal breaker, but so is waking up next to a corpse.

7. Just to reiterate: theoretically, yes, you're right, you are clean after a shower, but again, that cleanliness does not translate to the towel, especially after you have used it twenty times.

8. Never again list watching every single episode of *Law & Order* on Netflix as an "honor."

9. Keep the food in the basement *in the basement.* You will so eat something that expired in 2009 if it's the bona fide Apocalypse. (Don't worry, Anderson Cooper will let you know when that is.)

10. You have no street cred. If you want a second date, don't say things like "street cred." Ever.

11. Don't eat the leftover Mexican food you forgot was in the trunk yesterday when you find it today. Just because opening a hot trunk feels like opening an oven doesn't mean they are both equipped to incubate botulism.

12. Never clap at skunks in the garage to "scare them away."

13. If the milk has crust on the drinky part, go to your Drink Plan B. And when your fruit juice is bubbly like soda, chew something tangy-flavored to generate saliva if you are that thirsty.

14. You cannot wait out the smell in the refrigerator. The house will eventually be nothing but stink and rubble. The fridge will win. Every time.

15. If you can put your thumb through a piece of fruit, don't bite into it, although there is nothing funnier than watching you eat rotten food.

16. Which reminds me! If your back starts to hurt, unbutton your pants. Your waist hasn't been a thirty-two since you were in high school.

17. You blamed too much on Ambien Laurie and I let you because I needed to let her legend grow.

18. Never go into the attic. First, you are too fat to fit through the trapdoor. Second, there is *nothing* up there that you need. Third, there are monsters up there.

19. Drinking soda is not the same as drinking water. Your pee should not be the same color as a Ticonderoga pencil.

20. I lied. Lambskin is from lambs.

21. When your cousin's kids send you a graduation announcement, no, it isn't "just to let you know."

22. Despite the fact that it could feasibly work with the right positioning, thou shalt not ever clean the fireplace with a leaf blower.

23. If you discover your date is sneaking a bottle of water into the movie theater, do not put your hands on your hips and demand to know her plan "for when you get caught. In fact, *show* me the plan!"

24. Ovaries are not jazz hands. They cannot flutter and block unwanted things on demand, no matter what the frat boys say.

25. If you want a lady to love you, call Angelina Jolie's arms "pipe cleaners" again.

26. If you can toss the word "diaspora" into a conversation, back that smartness up by remembering to take out the trash (and remembering to bring it back in before you have to bring it back out again, despite the fact that you walk inches from it every time you leave the house).

27. You should not laugh when your next wife accidentally takes a dog pill and you are chortling so hard when you call poison control that the operator thinks it's a prank call.

28. So how did this work out? "I don't care. That's fine. That's fine. My next wife will think my story of reciting Jane's Addiction's 'Mountain Song' in my high school drama class is cool. Even if I didn't get to use the element of fire like I asked. She'll still think it's cool. Even though she will be way too young to know who Jane's Addiction is."

29. Remember when you said that if you ever got a chance to send a message from beyond it would be: "Frank Burns eats worms"? I'm going to try that, too. You will know that I'm watching you every time you hear someone behind a cash register say "Can I take your order?"

In closing, my dear husband, if you are still alive now, you've already beaten the odds, which means you only have 10,950 brushes with death to go, an average of one a day for roughly thirty years or so. I have tried to train you well, Grasshopper, and with this manual to guide you, I believe that you can live long enough to experience heart disease. I have faith in you. And remember, if anything tastes like it has bubbles in it when it shouldn't have bubbles in it, like cheese, you should probably stop eating it before you get sick and throw up in a soup bowl you grabbed instead of the trash can.

Love,
Your Dead but Still Concerned Wife

IF I ONLY HAD A BRAIN

$\mathscr{A}$lthough I played with the idea of reading a book this summer, I just don't think it's going to work out.

I know that's what all of my friends are doing; I bet every one of them is out there right now scanning the new-release tables at brightly lit bookstores, measuring one brightly colored clever cover against the one next to it, searching for books that look interesting: e.g., anything related to food or booze, any book with Tim Gunn on the cover, and discreetly jacketed, socially acceptable porn.

But when I thought about it, I realized all I really wanted to do this summer was sit outside and eat chips and dip. That's my idea of a good time, frankly, and it requires a great deal of focus. The last time I lost my concentration while feeding, I walked around with a chunk of refried beans on my boob until it was jammie time because people apparently thought it was an ugly, awkwardly placed brooch or, more likely, a snack for later.

Chips and dip require all hands on deck, and if I have one of those hands holding a book, chances are good to excellent that I will lose my focus and grow a bean nipple or at the very least wind up looking a little homeless by the end of the chapter. This is especially true if the book happens to be *Wicked* because that's the book I was reading that time when nobody told me about the turd on my shirt. I had just bought tickets to the show, so I decided to read the book first. It was all going well until I got to the munchkin/animal orgy where a little guy goes all cellie on a lion and my mug of *hot hot hot* coffee completely missed my mouth and hit my neck instead. And I am here to tell you that there is nothing quite like the experience of being over thirty years old and having cashiers look at you, with a blend of confusion and disgust as soon as they spot the hickey on your neck. It's the same face people make when they can't tell what smells so bad in the fridge but this experience comes with a visual when they picture which mug shot from Match.com it was who was sucking on your neck.

So, no. Reading is out for me this summer. Snacking takes precedence.

Besides, reading can make you blind if you do it too

much. It's totally true. Last summer I was outside reading *Auntie Mame* by Patrick Dennis (yes, the Auntie Mame of the 1950s Rosalind Russell movie fame and it's hilarious) when I looked up, and all of a sudden, everything went white. Initially I thought: *I knew I put too much salt on my lunch! Sandwiches don't even need salt! What the hell was I thinking?* But then, after I cried "Help!" several times and no one answered, even though the windows were open, my sight gradually returned and I saw my husband framed in the kitchen window, regarding me with a thoughtful expression—as if wondering whether or not I came with a return policy. I checked to make sure I had a pulse and then looked out the window to give my husband the thumbs-up even though he'd already walked away, when the blindness struck again.

"Damn it!" I said. "How many strokes can one person have in a day? It was just a little salt! It's not like I ate a Lean Cuisine! Plus, I had a vegetable yesterday!"

As soon as my vision cleared, I looked down at my book again and that's when it hit me: I was book blind. Scientifically, I don't know the specifics of the condition or what the medical term for it is, but I am pretty sure I saw a *Nova* episode about it. And what happens is: the rays from the sun streaming through the window reflect off the book page and char your retinas like a well-done steak, imprinting a photonegative of the page you were reading on the backs of your lids.

And I don't want that. I mean, I enjoyed the book very much, but the last thing I want to do is read the same page of *Auntie Mame* every night before I go to sleep, while "*Hurry with my tray, darling. Auntie needs fuel*," repeats on a loop in my mind. Maybe I'd be better off with an iPad, but truthfully, I see what a grease trap my iPhone is and I hate myself each time my french fry of a cheek leaves a rainbow effect on the screen. There's no way I can deal with an oil spill of that size. I'd have to keep a bottle of Dawn in my purse at all times.

These were all things I was telling my friend Sebastiane on the afternoon we had just returned from seeing *Wicked* and she asked me what I was planning on reading this summer.

"Nothing," I answered briskly. "I told you: I'm sticking to chips and dip. Reading almost made me blind. Do you know people thought I had a bean nipple?"

"So you're not reading anything?" my friend questioned suspiciously. "At all?"

"No, not one book," I confirmed, pulling *Auntie Mame* off the shelf. "But here is the one I was telling you about."

"Isn't that the one that blinded you?" Sebastiane asked.

"Yes, and I know page eighty-six by heart. I read it every

night while I'm waiting for my Ambien high to kick in, and it makes me cry with laughter."

Sebastiane squinted. "Were you on Ambien when you read the little-person sex scene in *Wicked*? Because, you know, that wasn't in the play. I kept waiting for the pygmy nudity, but even the flying monkeys kept their clothes on."

"I'm so glad that wasn't the page I was reading when I was book-blinded!" I informed her.

"So what books are you not reading this summer?" she asked.

"I just got a copy of Stella Gibbons's *Nightingale Wood*," I advised. "It was out of print for fifty years. You should read that and let me know how it is. And I just got a biography of the writer Jean Rhys called *The Blue Hour*. She goes to prison, abandons her babies, and then turns into a crazy, drunken landlady who attacks her tenants! That sounds so good. I think you should read that, too.

"Oh! Oh! Oh! *Americans in Paris* about expats who were caught in Hitler's invasion during World War Two and couldn't get out. Did you know that Sylvia Beach, the woman who owned Shakespeare and Company—the bookstore where every famous author hung out—was arrested and sent to live in the monkey house of the Paris Zoo during the occupation?

"Will you promise to read all of those books this summer and then tell me all about them?"

Sebastiane sighed. "I'll try," she agreed. "But I think you should just skip the chips and dip, stay inside, and read them yourself. You love reading! And you love central air, so really it's a win-win."

I shook my head. "I can't. I have a book due in September."

"Oh," my friend said. "I see. So the stuff about snacks, the fear about book blindness, the grease on the iPad—those were all lies? I know the iPhone part is true—why *is* your skin always so shiny?"

"I don't know but I have more creams and soaps and face scrub under that sink than the cosmetics aisle of CVS—that's not the point," I countered. "Did you hear anything I just said? Abandoned babies? Drunk landladies? *The monkey house?* You know if I start reading any of them, I won't be able to stop myself. And then I won't make my deadline. And then I'll have to get a job. And I don't like jobs."

"Right," Sebastiane conceded, and thought for a moment and then perked up. "I have an idea. Let's get a bib, some chips and dip, go sit outside, and make your reading list for September. And I'll bring all of the books home with me to remove the temptation."

"Deal," I said. "I'll make the margaritas."

Sebastiane looked at me disapprovingly, though I know she secretly wanted one, too.

"What? I'm thirsty," I explained. "I'll start writing tomorrow . . ."

WHO SAID IT WAS DONUT TIME?

I couldn't believe what I was seeing.

I hadn't seen anything like it since my little dog Maeby trotted into my friend Kartz's house, stopped, squatted, and deposited a compact, medium-size log in the middle of a giant white wool flokati rug. She was very officious about it, as if it were standard protocol for a dignitary visiting a small, primitive land that suddenly tapped a relentless supply of oil and knew it.

But I'm getting ahead of myself. First and foremost, let it be said that I've thrown a lot of parties. As a result, I've had experience with all sorts of party guests: the one who stays long after everyone who could have possibly offered him a ride home has left; the one who knocks a full beer all over your living room rug and simply watches—still standing in the spill, still wearing her Halloween pig mask—as you hunker down on all fours and try to sop it up; or the ones who help themselves to several bottles on the wine rack that weren't meant to be imbibed by already drunk people, especially those you've never met before.

As a hostess, I've learned that when you invite others—both strange and familiar—into your home, be as prepared as you would be for a Mongol invasion. Some people automatically assume that everybody rents her home, and that whatever you destroy, pee on, or set on fire at someone's house will be covered by a mythical security deposit.

I've also learned that a good offense is only as effective as the locks on your bedroom door, the level of childproof difficulty on the tops of your prescription bottles, and your ability to head off a situation before you're kneeling at Pig Girl's feet with a yellow dish towel in a scene plucked right out of a David Lynch movie.

However, I always thought that the act of hiding the after-dinner course was something that only happens on *Intervention* after the girl who gets hysterical when she sees a refrigerator counts out the six peas and four salt flakes she allows herself for dinner. Of course, you need to hide the good liquor and the Dilaudid that was the prize from your last kidney infection—*of course you do,* but donuts? Who the hell hides donuts? What kind of nut hides donuts?

Well, apparently, I do. Apparently I am the kind of nut who will put in the effort to camouflage the donut boxes with a stack of empty Tostitos and Lay's Potato Chip bags. I am that nut. Because I've learned from past mistakes that if you don't hide the three dozen donuts you bought from the best donut place on Earth, you never know what will happen.

You never know when you're going to walk into your kitchen with the last of the dinner plates cleared and see the last bite of a donut slide down the gullet of a forager who sniffed out the irresistible scent of a bacon maple bar with more precision than a cadaver dog, hours before you planned on serving them, despite an excessive amount of trash on top of the boxes *because you had a feeling*. You had a feeling that a certain somebody was going to wait until the kitchen emptied and the coast was clear to embark on a search-and-destroy mission to pick out the very best donut underneath all the fake trash and try to devour it like a crocodile inhales a wildebeest in the seconds you've been gone.

Legs and all. A crispy fried hoof shaped like a bacon strip still sticking out her mouth.

At least when I caught my dog acting like she was in a barnyard, she had the decency to look away when I pointed and gasped.

Now, before I describe how quickly the situation disintegrated, I think I need to explain that I was the one who called and placed the donut order; I was the one who selected the perfect combination out of forty-two possible flavors; I was the one who made the executive decision to end the night on a sugar high in perfect party harmony; I was the one who went downtown to pick them up, circling the block five times before I found a parking spot; I was the one who paid for them and then carried fifteen pounds of party harmony back to the car; I was the one who pushed them all the way to the darkest corner of the breakfast nook and placed every piece of detritus with excruciating precision and a subtle eye for disorder so as not to attract attention, much in the way a bear caches a camper with a flimsy tent. And on top of all that, I was the one who was called a "Stingy Pregnant Cow" when I didn't give the homeless ruffian on the corner a dollar for his trouble of getting enough face tattoos to render him unable to work at anything but creating a cardboard sign that says "I'll be honest: I'm gonna buy vodka with it."

All of that being said, I don't think that my stopping dead in my tracks and demanding "Who told you it was Donut Time?" was a particularly outrageous thing to do, although it did not prevent the offender from swallowing, then marching back to the other party guests and declaring that I had just yelled at her.

That was not yelling. *It was not yelling.* Everyone knows the Act of Yelling must include a hand movement in order for it truly to be classified as Yelling, which would be impossible, since both of my hands were firmly planted on my hips.

In the future, I have decided that party-goods camouflage is not a strong enough security system if Dog the Donut Hunter is prowling around your kitchen armed with a search warrant and a pair of handcuffs from the Spy Store. Clearly, a layer of garbage is not enough of a deterrent to stop some people from clawing through it, particularly if a pork product is somehow involved. I mean, hey, I smelled them, too, in the private quarters of my car. They were strapped into the passenger seat; they couldn't escape, but I stopped myself from digging in by envisioning party guests recoiling at the sight of donuts with thumbprints fossilized in the icing like the footsteps of early man stamped across a mud plain, or teeth marks scraped into the frosting like a beaver to a log. So I compromised and took the one on top without messing up anything to the side or below, *but I paid for them and I didn't even particularly like the one I took.*

In order to prevent another dessert attack from recurring, I realized I needed to draw up alternate plans. I thought about stashing the dessert items in a secure area, like my underwear drawer or the bathtub; although, truth be told, the bathtub has not proven to be such a sacred, restricted area in the past. The truth of the matter is, if someone's going to crawl into a dark corner and paw at trash in order to be the first (or second) one to snag a donut, only a surge of electrical current will stop them, and the clause in my homeowner's umbrella policy is a little vague for my comfort level.

I honestly don't know whether there's a solution to this problem, other than reverting to animal instinct and marking my territory with a litter box or a spray of coyote urine to discourage predators. But then the donuts would be ruined for pretty much everybody (believe me: there would still be at least one taker) and all that effort you put into attaining perfect party harmony through donut consumption will have been for nothing. But the next time someone discovers a donut box buried under trash in my Intentionally Dark Breakfast Nook, that person better look before fingering.

There just might be a fragment of a used flokati rug that I purchased from a friend with a little brown item deep inside the box that isn't exactly maple glazed.

YELP ME

All I really wanted to do was order a pizza.

That's all I wanted to do.

I didn't want to get into a sparring match with anonymous assholes on the Internet, I didn't want to argue about libel laws, and I certainly didn't want to enter a metaphysical debate concerning my entire existence with people who actually take time out of their lives to write a review of Olive Garden for fun and post it online.

Then again, that's what happens when you enter the arena of Roman-inspired public games on Yelp: before you know it, shut-ins who only venture outside to eat and then race right home to post their reviews are calling for your head on a flagpole.

Like I said, I was only planning to order a pizza from a

new Italian restaurant near our house. We had been there once before and the pizza was great—chewy crust, perfect sauce, mozzarella made by the owner every day. It was the closest thing to New York–style pizza in our neighborhood. And who doesn't like a great new pizza place? It's like discovering gold in your basement, or finding out that in the time it takes to pull on your Spanx, you will actually lose thirty pounds with a couple of deep breaths, some friction burns, and a sprained thumb—nothing but pure awesome as far as the eye can see—and *no one* has the right to mess with that.

But when I looked up the restaurant's phone number online, I was shocked to find the following words under the second Google listing: "I would NEVER eat at this place." It was the start of a thread on Yelp with numerous posts by people who had decided that although none of them had been to my new favorite pizza place, they were never going to try it because they were convinced that someone associated with the restaurant was posting phony positive reviews. And the Yelper bees were angry about it. Buzzing. Ready to sting.

"Goddammit, don't kill my new pizza place!" I cried at the computer screen. Since when is it a crime to post a positive review of a restaurant when you genuinely love the food and just happen to know the owner? I must have missed the paragraph in Revelations that says the last sign of the apocalypse is a nice review of a pizza place to cue Satan to step up and rule Earth for a while. Apparently, the phrase "the crust is good" was the wrong thing to say to people on the Yelp thread, and if you hadn't guessed by now, I was the one who said it.

Maybe they didn't like being called assholes—that was probably part of it. But seriously, what did all these people do before their life goal was to earn "elite" status on a message board because they went to six Starbucks in a two-mile radius and compared aromas? Were these the same people who subscribed religiously to *Reader's Digest* and constantly submitted their own jokes? Were they compulsive couponers? Or perhaps the kind of people who would spend way too much time attempting to draw Tippy the Turtle in order to get into a correspondence art school? Is this what happens to society when people don't have to use up spare time to darn their own socks or milk cows?

I don't know how many hobbies you have to try and suck at before you find your way to Yelp, but it appears to be an overwhelming number. True, I do know some people who contribute useful, informative content, but they aren't the ones organizing witch hunts and carrying torches to my favorite new pizza place. And, if I may be so bold, if you wanted to be a food reviewer, why isn't that your job? (Sorry. Blogs don't count. Really. They don't.)

Instead, Yelp has evolved into a socially acceptable bloodsport, and suddenly, it's perfectly fine to cast allegations out into the Google wind and have those accusations listed second on a results page. The first girl who came at me, Hannah "the Banana," immediately said that I was a fake person with a fake profile, and if that wasn't enough, she demanded: "Who r you? We r avid yelpers with numerous tips and photos and friends and reviews. I plan and go to events. I am elite."

And that was true. As a member with elite status, Hannah "the Banana" has climbed up the asshole rungs of the Yelp ladder, with such classic reviews as: Bed, Bath & Beyond ("The 20% off coupons you get in the mail, you can use them EVEN if they are expired!!"), Olive Garden ("WE GOT SOOOOOOOO SICK!!! I don't know what would make us that sick but now I really do NOT want to eat here ever again!"), and perhaps her Magnum Opus, 7-Eleven ("Good location. Always open . . . and there is a redbox outside so that's cool. If you try a slurpee my fav flavors are pina colada and banana . . . and even the two together . . . try 'em!") And, because I know you were waiting for this one, Hannah gave Subway four stars.

Ahhhhh. The elite.

So I replied to Hannah "the Banana": "You're the fake. You're not even a banana," and I begged her to review

T.J.Maxx. Well, clearly she rallied the troops of the elitist goon squad because soon, another elitist, Mary "the Skeptic," entered the fray. I'd written that it wasn't cool to assume that everyone who posted a positive review of the place was fake—that's when Mary announced that I was a fake, too.

The conversation proceeded just as you would have expected: a post from me suggesting Mary take a communications law class before spreading more libel about other area restaurants, another accusation from Mary that I wasn't a real reviewer but merely a plant from the restaurant. Honestly, I don't know how to argue my existence with someone who has reviewed a gas station (one star). I also don't know what someone who reviews a gas station expects from a gas station. I expect gas and to hopefully not die in a sudden explosion. If those two things happen, that's a winning experience for me. But surprisingly, once someone believes you are not a real person, it is remarkably hard to debate that you do indeed exist—especially when that person is so delusional they gave Applebee's four stars *twice*. Two different locations. That's diabetes squared. Both legs, sister.

Mary "the Skeptic" was such as elitist, in fact, that not only did she review the University of Oregon (three stars) and the airport (three stars), but she also blazed an elite trail by reviewing Yelp—yes, Yelp—itself. *Extraordinary*. Imagine Mary's disappointment, however, when she dropped into the home office in San Francisco and expected to be escorted upstairs to the main office because, as she explained to the receptionist, she's *elite*. You know, Elite. As in "I reviewed ten separate Starbucks and gave them all the exact same rating (three stars)" Elite.

Alas, maybe it was the four-star review of Red Lobster that finally caught up to her, or perhaps it was the general impression she gave of being a waddling lunatic who had just wandered in off the street, but Mary's request was denied. "When I tried to ask the receptionist whether I could go up to your headquarters to 'check in,'" Mary yelped. "She told me she had no idea what that meant." And thusly, two stars were dropped from what could have been an impeccable rating. In the end, Mary gave her host and, at the same time her denier, a "C."

So I decided that perhaps it was time for one more review.

Mary, "the Skeptic"
Category: Local Flavor, Active Life
Two Stars

Although Mary "the Skeptic" appears to be very real, her fact-gathering tactics could use some sharpening. Attention to detail is superb, spending what must have been at least a half an hour composing a review of the local sanitation company (four stars), which she called "somewhat reliable." Spends an inordinate amount of time eating meals with her mother-in-law. Delights in crinkle-cut fries and not surprisingly, has a special soft spot for restaurants that provide menus for people with dietary restrictions. Is bold—not afraid to write a review of a restaurant she has only walked into, or one that she's simply heard about. Like most Yelpers, has a tendency to force the mating of any word with the suffix "-ness," even if that merge is somewhat rough and/or confusing to the general population. Has a photo of every meal eaten since February 2011. Is not deterred easily, and truly believes she can determine the real from the unreal. Online social skills are somewhat lacking and could be considered "abrasive" or even "bossy" (although sodium levels are most likely quite high).

But please, Mary, "the Skeptic," continue in your elitist ways, carry on with your Yelp mission. Keep eating at the chain Mexican place you love so much (four stars!), especially since my plumber told me that their kitchen is so filthy he wouldn't drink a soda in a can from that place (which will remain unnamed since I did, in fact, take a communications law class).

YOU ARE NOT INVITED

I wasn't on the Facebook invitation list.

I checked twice, three times, sure that I was just so used to seeing my own stupid face that I had skipped it out of habit. The list was long, full of faces that I knew. A long line of faces that had eaten party food at my house and had pulled a beer I had paid for out of a cooler on my back porch. And on this long list of invitees to the birthday party of a person I considered a very good friend, my name wasn't there.

Mark Zuckerberg is an asshole, I immediately thought. The last thing I ever wanted in my life was social transparency! I want to stay in the world where I think that the people who like me like me and the people who hate me like me, too. I don't need to know the truth! I can't handle the truth. Who can?

If you ever really feel the urge to time travel, especially back to seventh grade, all you need to do is log on to Facebook. It will only be a matter of moments before the opportunity presents itself: people laughing in pictures that you're not in, inside jokes you don't get—proof that people you like don't like you back.

I was instantly transported to a place where I emerged from a lunchroom with smooshed bread packed around the orthodontics of every tooth. I'd already given up saltwater taffy, Cracker Jacks, and corn on the cob—for four years. *I was not giving up bread.* But, on the bright side, if I were back in seventh grade, it would be the last year I'd be able to wear buttoned shirts without the aid of safety pins in the breast bud area. I should really enjoy the moment because I have a decent body mass index at age twelve that will scurry out of my control by eighth grade due to my Nutty Ho Ho obsession.

Still, on Facebook, I can't help focusing on the fact that I have been left out again, by people I know, people I trusted.

I have two immediate reactions:

1. Wishing Mark Zuckerberg would get some friends—friends who will probably blow him off and scar him irreparably by the social burn he has witnessed from his very own creation turned monster.

2. Bursting into tears, putting on my KC and the Sunshine Band album, and rocking out while imagining Rick Springfield pushing the hair that I have put off washing all week off my face with a gentle, loving hand, wiping my tears away with the cuff of his red leather jacket, and hopefully not popping a pimple on my cheek in the process.

What did I do this time? I wonder, looking over the invite list again. Oh. *Oh, oh, oh.* I see *she's* invited, the girl who got drunk at a party last year, fashioned the cardboard twelve-pack holder into a hat and set it on fire; and look who else is coming, the guy who is clearly so on the spectrum he can make talking about Honey Boo Boo as tedious and snore-worthy as whatever he just read in *Harper's*. And the girl who got an $800 tattoo running up every fat roll on her right side, claims to be too poor to order anything off a menu but will help herself to food on your plate—she got invited, too!

How can I not be invited? If it was because I said you had cheap toilet paper at your house, I'm sorry. But I just don't understand why you wouldn't want your guests to have the best bathroom experience possible, and not have to go through half a roll of off-brand bathroom tissue just to accomplish the mission that four squares of Charmin easily can. You get what you pay for. I will buy meat in the clearance section before I will skimp on a life necessity like sturdy but gentle, nonballing toilet paper. And yes, I know you spent some time abroad and we should all be happy that we live in America where newspaper is upcycled in more primal ways than say, the Czech Republic. My point is that we *do* live in America, not in a country crippled by wars and huge moles. That's all. We live in America. Home of decent toilet paper. Wipe free or die.

Any yes, I will admit that I did walk away from your grandma midsentence at your last barbecue but she spit a taco chip on my face while she was talking and in all honesty, I stood there for as long as I could. *For as long as I could.* It landed right above my lip and it flew at me like a rocket. I knew it and she knew it, but did she reach over and wipe it off? NO. And was I too afraid to insult her by brushing a chunk of masticated grandma food off my face? YES. So I stood there, seeing the yellow chunk that seemed as big as the sun every time I looked down. I tried to blow it off. I tried to shake my head. But the chip had guacamole on it, the mortar of nature, and it was going nowhere. It would stay with me for decades if I let it. Three people passed by and pointed at my lip, including my husband, who yelled at me later for not being a good party eater.

And if my not being invited to this party had anything

to do with the stuffed mushroom incident, then say it to my face. I was the one who invented that recipe, experimented for years with blue cheese, garlic, and wine. THAT WAS ME. That was also me who gave you the recipe when you asked for it, that was me when a platter of them appeared at your Christmas party and a guest complimented you on them, and yes, that was me who heard you say "thank you," without giving me proper attribution. You cannot co-opt a stuffed mushroom and claim it as your own when I am standing two feet away. That is theft. Grand food larceny. You are an appetizer thief, and next time you ask me for the recipe for my chile con queso or mini-quiches, you can probably expect it to be an abbreviated list.

BUT I STILL LIKE YOU. AND I WANT TO COME TO YOUR PARTY. Why won't you invite me? I want to be the one to say to everyone after the girl with the flaming head has passed out that "*someone* needs an intervention, but she already ruined one of my carpets, so we can't have it at my house—although I will bring stuffed mushrooms." I want to tell the girl who has just plucked cheese off my plate that her tattoo doesn't look as much like an oak tree as it does a human, arthritic claw, and I am fully prepared to bring my own toilet paper. In fact, *I want to*. I insist on it.

I am the perfect guest.

I just don't want to talk to your grandma.

Stuffed Mushrooms

20 to 25 white or cremini mushrooms

½ to ¾ cup bread crumbs

1 shallot, finely chopped

2 to 3 tablespoons Parmesan cheese

¼ cup blue cheese

1 stick of butter, melted (yep, a whole salted stick—I love salt.
   Or you can substitute ½ cup olive oil.)

1 clove garlic, finely chopped or crushed

A glug or two of any white wine. ANY.

Salt and pepper, to taste

Preheat oven to 375ºF.

Clean mushrooms and remove stems. Chop up ten or twelve stems finely and mix with all ingredients. Fill mushroom caps until stuffing is about just over the rim of the cap. If you have some left over, fill them up more! Bake for 25 to 30 minutes. If someone asks you for this recipe, make sure they give you the goddamn credit.

BLACKOUT

*T*hat's it!" my mother snapped from the other end of the phone. "I'm not talking to you anymore. From now on, we are not talking!"

This was hardly the response I expected after giving my mother a compliment. I was stunned. No, I take that back. I was not stunned, but I guess I didn't expect that strong of a reaction.

"Did you hear what I said?" I reiterated, *positive*—no, I take that back—*hopeful* that my mother had heard me wrong when I told her that when I got notes back on a project I was writing, the first comment was: "More of your mother. Love her."

"You were their favorite part in the whole thing!" I tried to tell her. "They want more of you!"

"I heard what you said, and that's why I'm not talking to you anymore," she explained, her voice rising. "If I don't talk to you anymore, then you can't write about me anymore."

"That is ridiculous," I stammered. "Who doesn't want to be everyone's favorite part?"

"ME!" she shot back. "Why don't you write about your in-laws? They're funny."

"Are you kidding?" I asked. "That lineage is off-limits! Most of them have guns and I have to eat Christmas dinner with those people!"

"In that case, I'm buying the next gun I see on QVC," my mother informed me. "Even if it's not Joan Rivers's brand."

"See?" I said. "That's why you're everyone's favorite part."

"I don't know what the hell you're talking about. You have a weird brain. Why can't you leave me alone and write about little boys and girls like that other woman with the weird brain?" my mother asked.

I took a stab at it.

"You mean J. K. Rowling?" I answered. "The richest woman in the world? I do not have the same brain as J. K. Rowling."

"Well, maybe not the same one, but there's something wrong with both of your brains," my mother continued. "She's a weirdo. I heard there's a lot of sex in her new book.

Disgusting. You should try to write a magic book—one in which the mother is dead."

"I can't help it if you're funny, Mom," I tried to explain. "That's not my fault. That's God's fault."

"Don't blame God for that!" my mother snapped. "I am not funny. I just don't know why you couldn't have been a nurse or a paralegal."

"You're hilarious," I argued.

"Name one thing I said that was funny," she challenged me.

I cleared my throat and launched into my best Mom voice, complete with a thick Brooklyn accent. "'So I went for my first iPad class today, and there were ten people in the room. I was smarter than nine of them.'"

My mother waited for me to finish the joke.

"That's not funny!" she finally said. "They were all touching their screens, making them filthy, like little animals. Your father bought me a special pencil that I use. Why would you dirty your screen if you could just use a magic pencil? That's not funny. That's using your head!"

I launched into exhibit B, my second impression.

"'So I said to my friend Judy, "Here, this is the stupidest book I've ever read. You'll love it,"'" I finished.

Again, my mother paused.

"Oh," she said. "That James Patterson book. You know,

he is my favorite author. But that book stunk. It was terrible. And you know what? She loved it! Did I ever tell you Judy has a tattoo?"

"Yes," I confirmed. "Every time you say her name."

"You know," my mother said, pausing, "to think that I was so excited when you were born. When, in fact, I should have looked at you and said to myself, 'This is the one. This is the one that's going to kill me,'" my mother said. "Because I would have been right!"

"Well, if you're so unhappy with me, who would you trade me for?" I challenged her. "Any daughter in the world: who would you trade me for?"

She giggled a little bit. "You know," she said. "You know."

Now it was my turn to pause.

"Linda? You'd trade me for my sister Linda?" I asked.

"Sure," she said.

"No," I corrected her. "No. You're *trading* me, not eliminating me. You have to trade me for someone else. You can't just cancel me out."

"Are you sure?" she asked. "Because eliminating is fine, and I don't know what difference it makes."

"It makes a difference!" I yelled. "You can't trade me for a daughter you already have!"

"Maybe I can have two Lindas," she suggested. "Linda twins."

"Mom, pick one of your friends' daughters. Which one would you rather have instead if me?" I insisted.

"Ooooooh," she said, thinking. "I know! I know! Debbie, my friend Erna's daughter—I'd rather have her."

"Why?" I asked calmly.

"Because she takes Erna out to lunch all the time and even bought her carpet," my mother explained.

"I thought Erna lived in a studio apartment," I said.

"Yeah. So?" my mother replied.

"That's like buying someone a bath mat," I shot back. "Your house is five thousand square feet. I'm not buying five thousand square feet of carpet."

"Maybe that's why I'd rather have Debbie," she said smugly. "And maybe that's why I'm not talking to you anymore."

"Doesn't Judy have a daughter?" I asked.

"Judy with the tattoo?" she answered. "I don't know."

"All right, fine," I replied quickly. "So how do we work this new arrangement, what's the plan? Do we get a proxy to be our communication surrogate, or are you calling for a complete blackout?"

"A blackout," my mother decided.

"Even when I visit?" I asked. "The blackout is in effect when I come home, too? You're just not going to talk to me?"

"Yeah," my mother answered.

"Wow, I had this dream once!" I exclaimed excitedly. "So I say something to you, and you just stay quiet?"

"Yeah," my mother confirmed.

"Can we practice now?" I asked.

Silence.

"Entitlements," I whispered.

I heard her take a breath.

"Health care for everyone," I said a little louder.

She exhaled.

"Obama!" I said in a full voice.

"That's enough!" she cried.

"I am so wearing my Arizonans for Obama T-shirt when I get off the plane!" I exclaimed in joy, and I couldn't wait to tell my other sister, Lisa. "I bet Lisa's going to start writing about you, too!"

"Whatever," my mother replied. "I'll trade for three Lindas."

"So when does the blackout start?" I asked. "How will I know that you've started not talking to me?"

"I don't know," she said. "I have to think about it."

"All right," I said. "Will you call me when it starts?"

"Sure," my mother agreed.

"Because I don't want to miss it," I added. "I want you to tell me when you've stopped speaking to me."

"Okay, I'll call you," she confirmed. "Maybe Sunday."

"Sunday's good," I agreed. "I'll be here when you call."

"So I'll talk to you then to stop talking?" she asked.

"Yep," I nodded. "I'll talk to you then."

"Talk to you soon about not talking," my mother said.

"All right, Mom," I said, "we'll talk then."

REWINDING

A pack of werewolves in human form are gathered beneath a tree, circling the torn and bleeding carcass of a man they have all fed from. An older woman, her face drawn and sunken like a rotting apple, addresses another man, wounded and bleeding, and insists he feed from the corpse, too.

"Wait—" my friend Kartz says as she freezes the frame with the remote. "Do you care if I rewind that?"

We are lying on Kartz's bed with her standard poodle, Massimo, stretched out between us.

"Uh-uh," I reply, shaking my head. I don't care, just as I didn't care the time before that, or the time before that, or the time before that. We've been rewinding a lot. An episode of *True Blood* is only an hour long, but it's taken us at least that long to get halfway through the show.

"Are you going to put this in the book?" she asks me as she rewinds it too far before she hits play and we end up watching something we just watched the last time she rewound it.

"Probably," I admit, and with perfect timing, Massimo kicks me to make me give him more room. I scoot over a little bit.

We were at dinner one night about six months ago when she mentioned that she thought she was losing her memory because she met a coworker in the hallway and couldn't remember his name. I just laughed.

"Oh whatever, you take Ambien!" I reminded her. "I flew all the way to Idaho with a stop in Seattle and got a manicure and don't remember it. The only reason I know that at all is because I made the girl doing my nails stop and take a picture."

"Okay," she said, visibly relieved. "And it could be stress, too, right?"

"Of course," I reassured her. "You're starting a new school session and you have a ton of stuff to do to get ready for your students. This is always a big rush time for everyone at the university."

"Yeah, yeah," she agreed. "I have a lot to do. You're right. I'm not going to worry about it."

"Don't worry about it." I laughed and had a sip of wine.

"I won't," she said, and then paused. "But I forgot an appointment I made with this woman."

"Stress," I reminded her. "What was it for?"

"I don't remember." Kartz shrugged, and then pulled out her iPhone, swiping the screen with her finger. "Here. It was for yesterday. At six thirty. With someone named Melanie. Who is Melanie?"

I stopped but didn't put the wineglass down. I looked at her. Kartz has tremendous, beautiful ice-blue eyes, a color so pale that they almost seem transparent, like aquamarine. They were fixed on me. She was not going to look away.

"Melanie," I said, pausing and looking back, "is one of your best friends."

A few days later when I called Kartz, she said she had felt dizzy earlier and that she was trying to make an appointment with a doctor. She thought it might be some new medication she had been taking, and that the memory loss was probably related. I agreed, relieved, and when I called her back the next day, she said she was feeling fine and wasn't worried about it anymore.

On Saturday, I checked my messages during intermission at a play my husband and I were seeing in Ashland, where we were spending the weekend to celebrate our anniversary. We had dropped our dog, Maeby, off at Kartz's earlier that morning and I called before dinner to make sure everything was okay. Kartz had been feeling great but I was still a little worried, despite her protestations that she was perfectly fine.

But she hadn't called back. Instead, there was a voice mail from Tannaz, a professor in the art department who taught with Kartz. I couldn't hear the message, the noise in the theater lobby was too loud, but I could tell it was urgent and that something was wrong.

"Laurie," Tannaz said as soon as I stepped outside and called her back. "Kartz is in the hospital. She has a brain tumor. They're operating as soon as possible."

I looked at my husband. It was clear to him something bad had happened.

"What?" he mouthed, his eyes widening. "What?"

After we dropped Mae off that afternoon, Kartz was walking both of our dogs in the park across the street when she saw a tree that had been knocked down by a recent storm. She took the dogs back home, returned to the park, and dragged half of a twenty-foot-tall tree across the street to her backyard, deciding it would make good firewood. Then she went back across to the park to get the second half of the tree. It was there that she collapsed and regained consciousness sometime later, not knowing why she was hanging on to half of a dead tree in a park.

She got on her bike and rode to the urgent care, where they immediately asked her to hold both arms up in front of her. One of them was lower than the other. That was when they sent her to the emergency room, and the attending physician ordered a CAT scan.

When my husband and I walk into the hospital room, we aren't sure what to expect. I'd imagined a solemn occasion, or at least a scary one—the kind that makes everyone anxious. But past the door is Kartz, propped up in her bed with a multitude of pillows, and friends, like Melanie and Tannaz, surrounding her with Massimo on one side of the bed and her other dog, Rocky, snuggled on the opposite side. Those dogs go everywhere with her. On bike rides in a pull-behind trailer made for kids. On shuttles up to Portland. On flights to Los Angeles, where her sister lives. She asked her doctor to write a note, then she got them service dog ID cards with Massimo's and Rocky's headshots on them, taken at a passport photo place. They are laminated.

"How did you get them in *here?*" I laugh, not talking about Melanie and Tannaz.

Kartz waves her hand and laughs. "I said I wanted my dogs. So Tannaz went home and got them," she says simply.

Oddly, everything seems normal. Everything seems all right. It is going to be okay. *This is not going to be a big tumor,* I thought to myself. *Not at all. This is going to be a little one, if there is such a thing. This is going to be a Sheryl Crow kind of brain tumor, the kind that's manageable and just sits within your skull like a jelly bean. It doesn't move, it doesn't grow, it is just happy to sit there without causing trouble. This is not a glioblastoma,* I said to myself, *it is not.*

One day, several years ago, during a phone call, my nana started calling my sister a "he" instead of a "she." While there was no question about my sister's gender, we laughed when Nana caught her mistake, because she could often be kind of goofy. When it didn't stop and she replaced the word "cup" for "dish" and had trouble making sense out of anything that she read, we suspected ministrokes. My mother took her to a doctor who ordered a CAT scan. We knew by that night that she had a brain tumor.

And it was not a jelly bean. It was a glioblastoma, the kind that would kill Ted Kennedy the following year. I had never heard that word before. It's a mean sort of brain cancer, it swells and it grows and it sends out tentacles with hooks on the ends to establish cancer cells in every part of the brain, like a spiderweb. Like a mean spiderweb. And my ninety-year-old grandmother had it. She also had a choice: let it be, or undergo brain surgery and then chemo and radiation.

"No," she said quietly as the neuro-oncologist held the MRI film of her brain with a large white ball sitting right above her ear. "I don't want any of that."

So I am shocked when Kartz asks the nurse to bring up the MRI on the computer screen that is next to the hospital bed. There's no film anymore, it's all digital on a screen. And on that screen is a big white ball above Kartz's ear, the size of a golf ball.

But it's still too early to tell. There is still hope. It is not a jelly bean, but it may not be a spiderweb. It could still just be a nameless big white ball.

Kartz is scheduled for surgery the next day after her sister and family arrive. I am dumbstruck when I walk into the room and meet them for the first time. Nana is sitting next to the bed—or at least, she looks just like I remember my nana when I was a kid. I don't even realize it's not Nana for a moment until I understand that it's not possible, and then I am introduced to Kartz's sister, Maria. I want to hug her, and I do.

Kartz shows no sign of hesitancy when Maria and I see her in pre-op and she has the right side of her head shaved. It's been a week exactly since we had dinner.

"I am not worried," she assures the both of us, and laughs. "It's going to be fine. I know that. I just needed a haircut."

Then she lies back, looks at the ceiling, and is quiet.

The surgery doesn't take long; it takes much less time than any of us thought. We're not sure if that's good or bad, but we expected it to last into the evening. My husband and I had gone home to let Maeby out and had just backed out of the driveway to head back to the hospital when Maria called.

"The surgery is over," she says. "The doctor said he got it all. It's all out! She's not awake yet, but she's in recovery in ICU, which is normal."

I agree that it's marvelous news.

"The surgeon said by looking at it he can tell what kind of tumor it is, but they still need to do tests on it to make sure," Maria continues, repeating what her husband, Frank, is saying in the background. "He said it's a glio— What is it, Frank? It's called a glioblastoma."

We walk into the OR waiting room, which is vast, modern, and tries to look comfortable. I remember fireplaces everywhere. We see Maria's family sitting in a circle of puffy, stuffed, neutral-colored chairs. They look stunned. They have been crying. We have all been crying.

"I'm sorry," I say as I take Maria's hand, incapable of saying anything else. "I'm sorry."

When the bandage—which is just a square of gauze and tape—comes off, the suture is substantial. Shaped like a backward question mark, the incision winds from Kartz's temple to behind her ear in a wide, sweeping curve. The skin is puckered and fastened by staples, about fourteen of them, holding Kartz's scalp together. It is difficult to see at first, but it's startling what you can get used to in a matter of hours.

A chaplain comes into the room and sits on the banquette off to the side. Kartz thinks he might be the doctor, because we have still not seen the oncologist, presumably because the test results are not back yet. So she listens to him when he begins talking about the end of life, and what that means, and how different people feel different ways.

I try to catch his eyes to signal for him to stop it. *She doesn't know this, none of us really do, so you need to stop it with the "what does life mean?" talk,* but he never looks at me. He pats her on the leg, and despite all of what he has just said, this was the signal she needed to inform him, maybe a little briskly, that she may have had a brain tumor, yes. That part is right. But she has no intention of going anywhere, and Maria will tell you that, and Kartz points to her sister, and that woman over there—and Kartz points to me—will tell you that, too.

I just smile. And I nod.

The next morning, when I get to the hospital, a covered dish arrives on Kartz's bed tray and she is very excited.

"Look, look," she says cheerfully. "They let me order my own breakfast last night from a list."

"Ooooo," I say, putting my purse down. "What did you get?"

"I don't remember!" She giggles, then lifts up the silver cover of the tray to expose her carefully chosen meal of oatmeal and salsa.

We both recoil in horror, and then burst out laughing.

"I hope that part of your brain grows back fast," I say. "Or I'm going to get sick of sharing my food with you."

When the oncologist finally comes in, four days after surgery, the room is packed. Many of Kartz's friends are there, so many that there is only standing room. He is young, doubtfully young, and he walks in, introduces himself, and flips open Kartz's chart. He repeats everything we already know, *you had a tumor, size of a golf ball, on the right side* (we all nod and look at the massive backward question mark stapled into the shaved half of Kartz's head), and it's a stage-four glioblastoma.

Quick as that. He says it as quick as that.

"*Yes!*" Kartz says, and claps her hands with several tiny beats, and develops a wide, beaming smile. "That's great!"

The doctor looks stunned.

"No," he says, looking around the room. "No, I'm sorry. Stage four is the most progressive. It's not good. It's a terminal; this type of cancer is terminal."

She is stopped. Her clear blue eyes look at me. They look at everybody. The room is quiet, but Kartz won't let it be quiet and she points a finger at this young, clean doctor in his white coat, with that folder open, and with the precision in which he spoke, she says with assurance, "I am not going to die." This girl with half a marked and sutured head, my friend who is missing most of her hair, my friend who doesn't remember that she was once married, says carefully, and with balance, "I am going to live forever."

We all believe her.

When she comes home, her dogs are waiting; they have missed her. Her head is wrapped in a plaid wool scarf that looks exquisite, shielding the cut from the sun. The swelling has gone down and it already looks better. Flowers fill the dining room and living room and friends stop by, bringing their children. The house is full of babies. Kartz wants to hold all of them.

The noise is happy.

In the week that follows, there are appointments: appointments with oncologists, neurologists, appointments at the university, where she is an art professor, and repeated trips to the lawyer. There are much-needed ventures to T.J.Maxx, Kartz's favorite place. She buys more scarves, hats, and a shimmery sequined cocktail dress that she puts on as soon as she gets home. It is silver and brings out the color of her eyes. She wraps laces of chains, silver and gold, as well as rosaries, around her neck and wrists. She pulls on her black leather clunky boots. She emerges from her bedroom in this fierce sparkly concoction and announces that this is her battle dress.

During a trip to an imports store, she threads an inexpensive beaded necklace around her hand and tells the teenage cashier that she is taking it, calling out "Something borrowed, something blue!" as she leaves the store.

"Don't even ask me to take you to a bank," I inform her. "I don't want to end up with a red laser dot in the middle of my forehead."

"I did not shoplift," she insists. "I told the guy I was taking it and when I was cured, I would bring it back."

"Of course he didn't say anything!" I say. "You think a high school senior is going to mess with a shoplifter who's already got a zipper stamped into the side of her head? Even I'm afraid of you on one side!"

Maria spends most of her time on the phone, calling the University of California, Irvine, and the City of Hope in Los Angeles, trying to get Kartz into a trial study for brain cancer. It is understood that Kartz cannot stay in Oregon; she can't stay at home. She'll need constant care for a while, and Maria has the summers off from her job as a nurse at an elementary school.

Gamma knife therapy is an option at UC Irvine, but chemo and radiation are definitive. Gamma knife, we hear, has great results on most patients. We cheer and clap when we find out she's been accepted into the trial but that she barely skated in because the diagnosis is terminal.

Finally, we think. Terminal is finally good for something. It's good for gamma knife therapy studies and stealing shit from World Market.

She is still wearing her battle dress a week later, and we find escaped sequins all over the house. The dress is beginning to fall apart, but it is of no consequence. It's just the way it is. We find them on the dogs, in the couch, sprinkled in the kitchen. Shiny, minute pieces that Kartz leaves behind her, reminding us, reminding us that she is here.

They leave for California in a rented van that is so weighed down that Frank isn't sure he'll be able to make a turn in it. It is full of things deemed essential: a collection of pure white, immaculate towels; an enormous box of boots with three-inch heels that make Kartz feel taller; at least four heavy winter coats and three suitcases of sweaters; a king-size dog bed and photo albums. Figuring out what to take isn't hard. It is deciding what to leave behind that is impossible.

When I point out that she's not going to need sweaters in Southern California, that she won't wear coats, and that she should pack sensible shoes instead of her Coach boots, the only response I get is a suggestion from my friend, who can't remember my name and turns her head, now staple-free and with only a scarred ravine, that maybe I shouldn't say anything else and just let her pack what she wants.

And she is right. This is not the time for anything to make sense.

Half a year later, only the top of her head has hair, in a spiky salt-and-pepper strip. Radiation has left the sides a little fuzzy, but it looks good. Kartz opens the door to the house she left in the spring, and Massimo jumps on me and nearly knocks me down. She looks healthy. She looks great. She looks like herself. The gamma knife therapy has been a success; a wonderful, lucky success. Radiation is done, but there are still the aftereffects and the partial loss of vision in one of her pale blue eyes. Her memory is spotty, and there are still times when she looks at me for a moment and I know to say, "Laurie." Chemo is ongoing, and will be for a year. But the MRI is clean, no tumors, no traces of the spiderweb; it is clean.

Kartz is back home for a week, moving some of her stuff into storage before a friend rents her house for several months. It's also a test to see how well she does on her own, if it's possible that she might be able to live the life she left before the big white ball showed up on her doctor's computer screen. Tonight, we are having a slumber party—me, Kartz, and Massimo. We put on our jammies and climb into a big, antique bed and turn on *True Blood,* a television show that she has rediscovered lately. With the constant scene changes and cast of shape-shifters, vampires, panthers, fairies, and now the werewolves, it's hard for her to keep up with the ridiculousness of what's going on at any given moment.

And the truth is, I hate this show. It's complicated and silly and, much of the time, kind of stupid. But right now, when the only issue is to remember why one werewolf is eating another, it seems remarkably simple, as Kartz raises the remote one more time and rewinds it all again.

ACKNOWLEDGMENTS

$\mathcal{S}$o may thanks, so little time because I am already beyond my deadline, as usual.

First and foremost, a kiss, a peck, and a juicy thank you goes out to the readers, the readers, the readers. I love spending most of my days with you guys, running stuff by you, and waiting for the next moment in which you will make me laugh like the lady who shops at Safeway in a bathrobe and wears a blonde wig like a hat. I love you all.

To Tricia Boczkowski (I spelled that right on the first try. FIRST TRY!) for being the fine, delightful, and hilarious editor that she is. I'm lucky to fall into your lap, sister. Very lucky and I know it. Thank you to the tireless Jenny Bent as always; Bruce Tracy, Amy Silverman, Claire Lawton, *Phoenix New Times*, Lore Carrillo, and anyone else I beg, borrow, or steal from.

ACKNOWLEDGMENTS

Thanks to the cop who pulled me over for driving a half mile over the speed limit just so I would have to pay a fine; for all of the many, many assholes on Yelp; the cabdriver who mooned me with his huge, dirty buttocks; the poet who had a really shitty attitude; the poor little boy I tried to abduct; the people who I threw up in front of; the person who rummaged through my fake trash to find a donut; to the people who did not invite me to their parties; and the scallywags at *Antiques Roadshow*. I couldn't have written this book without you, and I hope I never see any of you again.

Many thanks to Kelly Kulchak and Kathy White, neither of which is a devil or an angel, but both of whom sit on either shoulder and insist that I can do it. If either of you need vast quantities of fat for butt or check plumping, know that I am your donor.

Thanks to my family, my husband, and my dog, Maeby, for making me get out of bed every morning and plop down at the computer. Hopefully, by publication time, you'll be speaking to me again for a short period of time until you read this book. I'm sorry, you are too funny to ignore. It's your own fault.

Awesomely,

Laurie

AUTHOR Q&A WITH LAURIE NOTARO

1. Ten books into your writing career, what have you learned about writing or how best to make readers laugh? Is there anything you do differently now?

With each passing book, I have more interaction and communication with readers, particularly online and with social media—and I think that is so important. I love knowing what makes them laugh, what they relate to, and whether something strikes a chord or not. When approaching a subject or a story, I have this wonderful resource, and the readers never, ever disappoint me.

2. Would you say that you're prone to finding yourself in situations that make for funny stories, or that it's your perspective on everyday incidents that makes them

funny? In other words, could you say a little about the source of your humor?

I have never thought that I was someone whom funny things happen to, because these occurrences aren't specific to me. I think these sorts of things happen to everybody, you just need to be keyed in to see them—and in many cases, appreciate them—for the brushes of tragedy that they are. For example, I offered some great pants that I can't fit into anymore to someone I know, but after she tried them on, she declined, saying, "Well, they don't fit—unless I gained a bunch of weight." Seriously. What are you supposed to say to that, "Well, maybe one day you'll be as fat as I was when I thought I was skinny"?

3. As you've gotten older the content of your books has shifted. How conscious are you of that shift? Do you roll your eyes at your younger self or look at her fondly?

Oh, I not only roll my eyes but I shiver so hard I'm afraid my skin might fall off in one humiliated heap. Thank God I was raised Catholic, and although I'm a fallen Cath now, I take a bath in my sin every day and I wisely refrained from spouting some of the most questionable material I could have written about. Some of those pieces were written twenty years ago. I dare anyone to not be horrified of their 1992 selves. I dare them.

4. Do you write with your audience in mind, or tell a story like you're trying to make a certain person laugh? How conscious are you of your reader—male or female, young or old, etc.?

I have to make myself laugh first, and then if I do that, I feel comfortable passing it on for public consumption. As a writer, you know when you do work that is awesome, and you know when you are sucking, so I try not to suck. But I don't have a particular reader in mind when working; I think it's more of a reader's mindset than it is an age or gender. Your life experiences will dictate if you will understand why it is funny when I accidentally racially profile a youngster and try to buy him with a bottle of water or not.

5. How long does it typically take to gather enough material for an essay collection? Do you reject some pieces as "not funny enough" or otherwise not right for the book?

Oh, usually a year to two years. Some of the material in *Potty Mouth* was stuff that needed to be digested for years before I was ready to put my name on it, like the title piece. I needed time to see if I was overreacting or if my arch-nemesis in that piece was really a super asshole. Turns out, he's a super asshole. So I wrote it. Others I know right away, and I have it framed and ready to go. So it depends. They tell me when they're ready to go.

6. In this book you often focus on strangers and their bizarre and rude behavior, and after reading about them one can only conclude: What's wrong with people?! Is it simply part of the human condition to sometimes be unaware of or unconcerned with our own strangeness?

My theory is that everyone is crazy, it just takes the right circumstance to expose how insane we really are. The terrifying thing is that I have lost my fear of strangers, and before I even know what's happening, I am asking the guy who made my taco and is just letting it sit there for five minutes while he works on the order of the lady behind me, "Um. Dude. What do we need to do to complete this transaction?" And then, he looks at me like I'm the insane one. Like my taco hasn't already entered the second stage of decomposition because it has been sitting on his side of the counter for so long. That happened yesterday. Boo for Mucho Gusto. Boo!

7. Your husband and friends feature prominently in some of your stories. Are there instances where your family or friends draw the line or declare a story off-limits to the public?

Oh, my mother said she was going to stop speaking to me a month and a half ago because she didn't want to be in any more books. So I wrote about it, and I put that conversation in this book. Then she read that, and really did stop speaking to me. Last week, she asked if I was coming home for the holidays, and I said I didn't know because she wasn't talking to me. She shot back that it wasn't true. I reminded her that she hadn't called me in six weeks. She replied, "Well, that wasn't because I wasn't talking to you. It was because nothing happened." I give her until this book comes out, then she'll be mad enough to cut me off again. But I'll just write about that. She clearly doesn't understand that even if she stops speaking to me, she's still giving me material.

8. Speaking of off-limits, can you tell us about the first dead body now? Please?

I checked again. He said no. I promise, the first indication that the scab has fallen off, I'll hit the keyboard. But until then, I have to respect his Finder of the Corpse rights. I told thousands of people in the last book that as a boy, he had a tampon collection. I'm going to have to let this one lie.

9. Looking back, what was worse: human feces in your garden, vomiting on yourself in public, or discovering

that your puff was public property? Is self-inflicted grossness worse than coming into contact with that of others?

Definitely the vomit. Definitely. I really tried to die that day. I mean, it's the fear we all have, it's the worst thing you can do, and now, I've done it. I've peaked. I'm terrified for what's waiting for me next, and I just pray it doesn't include a toilet out in the open in Grand Central station. Seriously. What other landscape is open to me? I've traversed every humiliating terrain there is. That is a scary thought.

10. The last essay is a bit of a departure in tone, but it's a beautiful story. What prompted you to include it?

I included it because even in the darkest of circumstances, humor got us through. It was only because we were able to laugh at aspects of what was going on—in this case, the diagnosis of a stage four brain tumor in one of my best friends—that we were able to hold it together and even make it through those weeks. Without that perspective, I can't imagine what would have happened. It showed me that humor is such a vital mechanism in dealing with the good things in life and the truly terrible, and it's such an essential part of being human and coping. I wanted to show that despite the grim baseline of that piece, we laughed because we needed to. Because we had to.

11. In an interview, you mentioned being flattered that you were once compared to Erma Bombeck. Who do you think some of the funniest lady writers are these days?

Ha ha ha. Well, I don't read a lot of contemporary humor of my counterparts, I worry about seepage, crossover, and raw jealousy! But I will tell you which lady writers are absolutely hysterical. I'm in a phase where I'm mainly reading 1930s fiction from American and English writers, and those who I find particularly impressive are Margaret Halsey, Nancy Mitford, Stella Gibbons, and Anita Loos. All of them have made me laugh out loud and consistently. And the funniest book of all time, in my opinion, is *Auntie Mame* by Patrick Dennis. A resolute masterpiece, that book!